7/13/18

BELIEVE IT

BELIEVE IT

MY JOURNEY OF SUCCESS, FAILURE, AND OVERCOMING THE ODDS

NICK FOLES

WITH JOSHUA COOLEY

TYNDALE
MOMENTUM®

The nonfiction imprint of
Tyndale House Publishers, Inc.

Visit Tyndale online at www.tyndale.com.

Visit Tyndale Momentum online at www.tyndalemomentum.com.

TYNDALE, *Tyndale Momentum*, and Tyndale's quill logo are registered trademarks of Tyndale House Publishers, Inc. The Tyndale Momentum logo is a trademark of Tyndale House Publishers, Inc. Tyndale Momentum is the nonfiction imprint of Tyndale House Publishers, Inc., Carol Stream, Illinois.

Designed by Dean H. Renninger

Published in association with the sports agency Athletes First.

For information about special discounts for bulk purchases, please contact Tyndale House Publishers at csresponse@tyndale.com, or call 1-800-323-9400.

ISBN 978-1-4964-3649-8

Printed in the United States of America

24	23	22	21	20	19	18
7	6	5	4	3	2	1

To my wife, Tori; my daughter, Lily; and of course, our furry child, Henry. I am grateful beyond words for all of you, especially my wife, Tori—you are my heart and soul, and you motivate me to be better every day. Thank you for constantly believing in me and being there for me to lean on in the tough times. Lastly, thank you for your countless hours in helping to make this book as special as possible.

CONTENTS

FOREWORD

"Where did he come from?"

It's an easy question to ask in the wake of Nick Foles's amazing playoff run in the 2017 season. In other circumstances—or from the sidelines—I might have asked it myself.

When we suddenly lost our starting quarterback right before the playoffs, much of the sports world was convinced we were done.

But we knew Nick Foles. We knew where he came from. And we knew he was ready to play the game.

So when Nick led our team to an incredible Super Bowl victory and stepped into the national spotlight as the MVP, those of us who had worked with him weren't the least bit surprised. It's the rest of the world that was stunned, asking, "Where did this guy come from? How did he do it?"

I got to work with Nick for only one season. But in the football business, time is like dog years: a year in the football trenches feels like seven anywhere else. Nick has a sense of confidence tempered by humility that every football coach looks for in a leader. That combination stems from the fact that he's secure in his own identity. On the football field, he's one of the best quarterbacks in the NFL, and he has proven twice—on a very big stage—that he can play at an elite, championship level. And as a follower of Christ, he knows that his first job is to serve others, which makes him a great teammate—on the field and off.

As for humility . . . even as I write this, Nick still doesn't know where he's going to play next year. In fact, he may end up being the first guy ever to go from Super Bowl MVP to a backup role. A lot of guys would gripe and complain about that change of fortune, but not Nick. Whatever he's called to do and wherever he's called to work, he's going to be all in, 100 percent. More than anything, what he cares about is serving the Lord and making an impact for good. Wherever he is, he's going to pursue excellence.

In many ways, Nick's role this past season has been reminiscent of the story of David in the Bible. When David had to face off against Goliath—an ordinary man against an intimidating, larger-than-life foe—David likely thought, *Hey, killing this giant isn't going to be a big deal. I've already killed a lion and a bear. Been there, done that—let's go.* In that spirit, the idea that anyone would be surprised or shocked by what Nick did is downright comical.

Heading into the 2017 postseason, Nick had an unbelievable track record. He'd already thrown twenty-seven touchdowns in a single season, played in a Pro Bowl, and had countless other successes. He'd proven his skill and his character time and time again. When it came to football, he'd killed his lion and his bear.

So in Super Bowl LII, in the biggest game of his career, with the whole world watching, Nick took a chance. He pulled out his slingshot and ran the Philly Special—a risky trick play—and he defeated that giant in front of everyone who had underestimated him.

Above all else, Nick is a man of faith, and his faith is what gives him both his confidence and his humility. It also makes him dangerous. There's a quote from C. S. Lewis's Narnia series that describes Aslan the lion this way: "Who said anything about safe? 'Course he isn't safe. But he's good." God isn't safe. But he is good. So why should we mere humans play it safe? There should be a boldness and fearlessness to our actions and our speech. Sometimes we think it's dangerous to make a move or take a new job, but we also know it's just as dangerous to do nothing.

Nick's faith, confidence, and humility made him dangerous in the Super Bowl—and they're what make him a winner every day in everything he does.

Frank Reich
SUMMER 2018

PROLOGUE

Everything in my life changed in the span of sixty seconds.

It was March 10, 2015, the official start of the NFL calendar. The 2014 season was already a distant memory, which was fine by me. After enjoying a record-setting second season with the Eagles in 2013, I had regressed some during my third season. My accuracy wasn't as sharp, and my overall statistics were nowhere near my earlier Pro Bowl level. To make matters worse, I had suffered a broken collarbone in a week eight win over Houston and missed the rest of the season.

Nevertheless, I was filled with excitement heading into 2015. Despite my statistical drop-off the year before, I had led the Eagles to a 6–2 record, and we had a solid core of players returning to a 10–6 team that had barely missed the playoffs. My collarbone had fully healed, and I was feeling better than ever. Hope abounded.

That morning I headed to Equinox, my off-season gym in Irvine, California, to play some basketball and work out. I had been a decent high school basketball player in Texas, and it was always nice to dust off those skills between NFL campaigns. I felt fluid and sharp as I played a little pickup and a couple of rounds of H-O-R-S-E with some gym buddies. Steph Curry's roster spot was by no means in jeopardy, but I *was* nailing some pretty crazy half-court shots. Everything was clicking.

Eventually the weight room beckoned. The earbuds went in, the country music went on, and the volume went up. (You can take the country boy out of Texas, but you can't take Texas out of the country boy.)

I was in the middle of a set of leg presses when my phone rang. Typically I don't answer my phone during workouts, but the caller ID read *Chip Kelly*, and when your head coach calls, you answer.

The regular season had been over for ten weeks. My last conversation with Chip had been our exit meeting in early January before I left for the off-season. I assumed he wanted to check on my collarbone and my overall progress—maybe even discuss his roster-building plans.

Boy, was I wrong.

The call started out benignly enough. "Hey, Chip. What's up?"

"Hey, Nick. How are you feeling?"

"I feel great. I'm in the best shape of my life." And I meant it. "I'm really excited about this season and this team."

Chip told me he was happy to hear that, and then he talked a little about how the team was building for the future. Then, out of nowhere, came the fifty-foot swell.

"Nick, I'm actually calling to tell you that we've traded you to the St. Louis Rams for Sam Bradford. I wanted to be the one to let you know. Thanks for all you've done for this organization and for me personally. I wish you the best of luck."

Chip's tone was steady and measured—almost Belichickian—a stark contrast to what I was feeling. I stood up, faced the window, and blinked, unable to find words.

I'd loved playing in Chip's rapid-fire offense. We had so many dynamic weapons on the team—Riley Cooper, Zach Ertz, Jeremy Maclin, Jordan Matthews, LeSean McCoy, Darren Sproles. Besides, my wife, Tori, and I had quickly grown to love the city of Philadelphia, and we were excited about diving into community work there. We wanted to plant deep roots.

Now those dreams were being dashed in a matter of seconds. I was flabbergasted. What was I supposed to say? Like Barry Sanders in the open field, eloquent words escaped me.

"Well," I stammered, "thanks for the call. Obviously I want to be in Philly, but I understand."

Did I?

With all the graciousness I could muster, I said, "I'm truly grateful for my time with the Eagles. I wish you the best."

Chip informed me that I'd be getting a call from Rams head coach Jeff Fisher soon. Then we hung up.

I looked at my phone. The call had lasted exactly one minute. I stood frozen at the leg-press station, my body numb. Off-season trades are commonplace in the NFL, but you never think it's going to be you.

What just happened?

One moment I was planning my future as the franchise quarterback for the Eagles. The next, my world was like a merry-go-round flying off its axis.

Sure enough, Jeff Fisher called a minute later to welcome me to the Rams. I tried to sound enthusiastic, but honestly I was faking it.

After we wrapped up the call, I ditched the rest of my workout.

Whatever motivation I'd had that morning had evaporated. I called home and broke the news to Tori; then I called my dad.

The next day Tori and I flew to St. Louis to meet my new coaches, undergo a physical, and hold a press conference.

For the first time, I started to grasp a harsh reality: the NFL was a business, and I was an expendable commodity.

Everything I'd been working toward in Philadelphia had suddenly been stripped away.

None of this was part of my plan.

CHAPTER 1

DEFINING MOMENTS

People have been trying to define me throughout my entire career.

I'm *the guy*. I'm not *the guy*.

I'm mechanically sound. I'm too slow.

I'm able to light up a scoreboard. I'm a game manager.

I'm a building block. I'm a stopgap.

I'm a franchise quarterback. I'm an insurance policy.

I'm a Pro Bowl MVP. I'm a career second-stringer.

I'm dependable. I'm a fluke.

I'm a Super Bowl MVP. I'm trade bait.

I've been overlooked, praised, questioned, lauded, labeled, celebrated, and derided—sometimes all in the span of a single week.

That's life in the NFL.

From the moment you enter the league, everyone wants to slap a label on you—some tidy description of what they think you bring to the game. And more often than not, that tag sticks with you, regardless of whether it's accurate.

Most recently, I've worn the label *backup*, which, unfortunately, is fraught with negative connotations. Nobody aspires to be a backup. And although I take great pride in the supporting roles I've played in both Philadelphia and Kansas City, part of me still cringes every time I hear myself described that way. Not only is it limiting and one-dimensional, it doesn't come close to describing who I really am.

It took me years to separate Nick Foles the person from Nick Foles the football player. It was a long and, at times, painful process—in fact, I still struggle with it. But making that distinction has completely transformed my heart, my career, my perspective, and my life.

The journey hasn't always been easy, and I've made a lot of mistakes and missteps along the way. But looking back, I can honestly say that I wouldn't change a thing. Because at the end of the day, the lessons I've learned from my failures, struggles, and weaknesses have made me who I am today.

TEXAS TOUGH

For me, the road to the Super Bowl started—quite literally—the day I was born. I had barely even opened my eyes when my dad wedged a toy football into my pudgy little hand and snapped a photo . . . because that's what Texas dads do.

I grew up in Austin, home of the Longhorns, deep in the heart of the most football-crazed state in America. Come fall, at high schools all across the state, those Friday-night lights shine big and bright over packed-to-capacity, multimillion-dollar stadiums that would make even a few NFL teams green with envy. And when I say "packed to capacity," I'm talking anywhere from ten to twenty thousand rabid high school football fans, cheering, screaming, praying, and loving on their teams . . . because that's what Texans do.

I played high school ball at Westlake. By Texas standards, our stadium was on the modest side, seating just over ten thousand.

Before I got there, another Texas native, Drew Brees, led the Chaparrals to a perfect 16–0 record and a state championship, and he set records for passing yards and touchdowns that stood for almost a decade. Drew was already a Pro Bowl player in his third season with the Chargers by the time I was taking snaps at Westlake, but his legend loomed large.

I was a multisport athlete, lettering in both football and basketball. And I don't like to brag, but at six foot five, my shadow loomed about six inches larger than his on the basketball court.

I played power forward on the varsity team for three years, and while I was no LeBron, I could hold my own. I was tall and lanky, and I had a decent vertical leap and a pretty good shot. I was a lot faster and more explosive on the court than I was on the football field.

I earned an MVP and all-district honors in basketball my sophomore and junior years, and I even received a scholarship offer from a Division I school. But as much as I loved the game, deep down I knew I had a better chance of making it to the next level in football.

My football coaches, however, weren't sure I was tough enough to make it at first.

During my junior and senior seasons, I led Westlake to the 2006 Division 1 state championship game and broke the record for career passing yards (5,658) and touchdowns (56). But playing two high-impact sports takes a toll on the body, and I was almost always fighting off some kind of injury. The worst one happened my senior year. We had just closed out a long, grueling season where I'd thrown for nearly 3,300 yards, and six days later I had to play in a basketball tournament.

Early in the football season, I'd torn my labrum three-quarters of the way around, and I played a dozen more games with the injury. Needless to say, my right arm was shot. Because of the quick turn-around time, the coach had planned to rest me for the first couple of games. Then a couple of our guys got hurt, and he had no choice but to put me in.

I started off strong. I made a few jump shots and even managed a couple of dunks. Then, in the middle of a behind-the-back pass, my right shoulder completely gave out. The pain was excruciating. I doubled over, and when I glanced down, I saw that my right arm was just hanging there like a limp noodle. I looked at the bench and, with my good arm, motioned to Coach Faulkner to take me out of the game.

That torn labrum really knocked me for a loop. Not only did it cost me my final basketball season at Westlake, but it set me way back in my preparation for my first year of college football.

Still, I figured if Drew could come back from his injury to play at an elite level, so could I . . . because that's what Texans do.

It was months before I could even pick up a football, but I knuckled down and powered through my rehab exercises. That spring, at my senior awards banquet, the same coaches who had questioned my ability to make it at the varsity level told a packed auditorium that I was one of the toughest players they'd ever seen—not because of what I'd done on the field, but because of the way I'd fought back from my injuries.

PLAN B

Something else had happened while I was recovering from my shoulder surgery. Midway through my junior year, I was recruited by Dirk Koetter at Arizona State, and I made a verbal commitment to play football there.

I felt a real connection to Coach Koetter, and I thought the offensive scheme Roy Wittke was running under him would be a great fit for me and my "air it out" style of play. I liked the idea of going to school in a place with no real winter, and I had family in the Phoenix area. It seemed like a perfect fit. Then, right around the time we were getting ready for the state championship game, Coach Koetter was fired. As is often the case, his entire coaching staff went with him.

Even though my scholarship offer was still intact, the relational connection I had committed to wasn't.

I've always been a relational guy. Football is football. You can play anywhere. For me, it's the people I'm playing for and with that make all the difference.

After I had my surgery, I met with Coach Koetter's replacement, Dennis Erickson, who had come over from the University of Idaho. He made it clear that there was still a place for me at ASU, but I just didn't feel the same connection to the program that I'd felt with Coach Koetter. So that February, I officially decommitted from Arizona State and signed on to play at Michigan State under Mark Dantonio.

Mark is a great guy and a fantastic coach. I assured him that I was going to do everything in my power to be game ready come September. I continued to rehab my shoulder, and by the time I left Austin, even though I was nowhere near 100 percent, I was ready to take the Big Ten by storm. I was young and confident, and I had no idea what I was getting myself into.

Shoulder reconstruction was like a walk in the park compared to my first year in East Lansing.

SPARTAN CONDITIONS

That first Michigan winter hit me like a snow shovel. For that matter, so did the Big Ten coverage packages.

I pored over my playbook and tried to soak up as much information as possible, but the leap from high school to college ball was a lot more intense than I'd expected.

At quarterback meetings, Kirk Cousins, Connor Dixon, Brian Hoyer, John Van Dam, and I would sit and watch film, and Dave Warner, the quarterbacks coach, would look at me and say, "Foles, what coverage is this?"

I had no idea.

"Cover three?" I'd guess.

"Wrong," he'd shoot back. "It's cover one."

Sigh.

It's not that I hadn't seen coverage packages before. We ran schemes at Westlake just like everyone else. But I tended to play more by instinct. The more I struggled in meetings, the less confident I felt. And as a quarterback, once you lose your confidence, it's over.

And man, did my confidence take a hit across the board. Not only was I still recovering from shoulder surgery, but I was also more than a thousand miles away from home in a completely foreign environment. I had no family around me and not a single Texan in sight, and I had no idea what I was doing in position meetings. On top of all that, I was fighting for second string.

I only saw the field once that season, in a game against Alabama–Birmingham. Considering my arm wasn't quite 100 percent, I fared pretty well, completing five of eight passes for 57 yards, but make no mistake, I was still the low man on the totem pole.

Making matters worse, my high school sweetheart and I had broken up, and every time I logged on to Facebook, all I saw were pictures of my friends back home—smiling, suntanned, and having the time of their lives at Texas A&M, Baylor, UT, and TCU. Meanwhile, I was grinding it out in the weight room, on the practice field, and in the classroom from 6 a.m. to 10 p.m., all the while trying to figure out how to survive my first bone-chilling Midwestern winter.

At one point I called home, ready to throw in the towel. "Dad, I can't do this."

My dad is a tough guy. He never graduated from high school. His parents split up when he was young, so he had to help raise his brother and sisters. He has worked hard his entire life, and as far as I know, he hasn't complained once. In short, he's not a quitter.

So when I told him I didn't think I could hack it, he said, "Stick it out through the spring. If you still don't want to be there, you can transfer. But if you walk away from MSU one season after decommitting to Arizona State, you run the risk of never playing football again."

I was quiet for a minute, letting his words sink in.

"Okay," I told him. "I'll stick it out through the spring."

Things didn't get any better. In fact, they got worse.

Within a span of a few weeks that year, both of my grandmothers passed away. Losing a loved one would have been difficult enough if I'd been surrounded by family and friends, but going through it alone on top of everything else I was dealing with put me over the emotional edge. One night I was sitting in my truck, and I broke down crying.

I grew up in a Christian home, and my mom, in particular, is a really strong Christian—always helping people, putting others first, and never seeking attention for herself. We went to church as a family most weeks, but to be perfectly honest, most Sundays it was all I could do to stay awake. I knew who Jesus was, but I had never made the kind of commitment that my mom had.

Among other things, Mom was a real prayer warrior. Whenever she was struggling, she would pray to God for strength and guidance and for his will to be done. And no matter what happened—good or bad—she found peace in that.

So that day I followed her example. "God," I prayed, "I don't have any strength left. I don't have any confidence left. I have no clue why I'm in Michigan right now, but I have to believe I'm here for a purpose. I believe you have a plan for me. I trust you more than I trust myself, so I'm giving everything over to you. I can't do this on my own."

It probably wasn't the most eloquent prayer ever uttered, but it was sincere.

The next day I dug out the little travel Bible my mom had given me. Even though I'd had it for years, it still looked brand new. I started carrying it with me everywhere and read it whenever I had a few free minutes. By the time second-semester finals rolled around, that little Bible was as dog-eared, underlined, highlighted, and note-filled as my literature textbook.

I didn't understand everything I was reading, but just knowing that I wasn't alone—that God had a plan for my life, even if it wasn't clear to me yet—changed my perspective immeasurably.

I started praying for guidance about my future. Was I supposed to stay at Michigan State, or did God have something else in mind for me? As much as I tried, I just didn't feel settled there. I loved playing for Coach Dantonio, and I genuinely cared about all the guys on the team, but I felt like a fish out of water. If I was going to have any shot at being the kind of student athlete I believed I had the potential to be, I couldn't see it happening in Michigan. I had to get back to an environment I was comfortable in—somewhere I belonged. I needed the heat. I needed the sun. I needed to be around other Texas boys.

My dad's warning still echoed in my head, and that semester I had plenty of sleepless nights worrying that he was right. Without a doubt, it would be a risky move to walk away from MSU. But I'd been praying about it for months, and eventually I knew what I had to do. By the time I sat down to talk to Coach Dantonio, I felt genuine peace about my decision.

Looking back, it would be easy to characterize that year in Michigan as a failure. I was hurt and homesick, and I didn't see much playing time. When it came to my confidence level, I'd never been lower. But truth be told, that was actually one of the best years of my life. There were a lot of bumps along the way, and those experiences exposed some of the weaknesses in my character. But those challenges also put me in a position to grow in my faith, which in turn made me stronger and more confident than I ever would have been had I not gone through those tough times.

When I walked away from Michigan State, I had no doubt that God had a plan for my life. Now I just needed to figure out what it was.

TURNING UP THE HEAT

As soon as I got home, I started reaching out to all the colleges that had expressed an interest in me before I committed to ASU, but this time I limited my search to schools closer to home. These weren't big universities—they were small local colleges. I didn't care where I ended up as long as it was close to home and I got a chance to play.

Things didn't start off well. One school told me I was too big; another told me I wasn't their type.

Just as I was starting to get a little panicky, I got a text from Sonny Dykes. Sonny had recruited me when he was at Texas Tech, and now he was working as offensive coordinator under Mike Stoops at the University of Arizona.

The good news was they were interested in me. The bad news was they were all out of scholarships.

I wasn't in a spot to be choosy, so I decided to take a leap of faith and join the team as a walk-on. Granted, Tucson wasn't exactly next door, but I'd spent enough time in Arizona to know that I liked it. It also didn't hurt that I'd been a huge fan of Arizona's basketball team when I was growing up. Their football program hadn't made me an offer when I was in high school, but given my current situation, I decided not to hold that against them.

By the time training camp rolled around, my shoulder had completely healed, and my passing strength was back to 100 percent. It felt great being back out on the field with the sun beating down, hitting receivers in stride twenty-five, thirty-five, fifty yards downfield. There was no doubt about it: I definitely wasn't in Michigan anymore.

About a week into training camp, Coach Stoops called me over to the sideline. "Just so you know," he said with a smile, "you *will* be getting a scholarship come January."

I was ecstatic. It had been a tough road, but things were finally starting to turn around.

That's when I got blindsided.

I was walking up the stairs to get my sports physical at the McKale Memorial Center when the most beautiful woman I'd ever laid eyes on walked out of the weight room.

She had gorgeous brown eyes and long, dark-brown hair that was pulled back in a ponytail. She had an athletic build, and she was wearing a gray University of Arizona volleyball T-shirt. But it wasn't just her physical appearance that caught my attention. It was the way she walked, the way she carried herself. That confidence, combined with her looks—well, she took my breath away.

I didn't know who she was, but I was determined to find out.

As soon as my physical was over, I called my dad.

"Dad," I blurted out, "I just saw the most gorgeous girl I've ever seen in my life." I leaned against the cinder block wall, an enormous smile spread across my face. "I think I'm going to be okay here."

And you know what? I was.

I redshirted my first year, then took over for Matt Scott mid-season in 2009. I had a pretty decent year, throwing for 2,486 yards and nineteen touchdowns, which was good enough to guarantee me the starting position in 2010.

My junior year got off to a great start. We were 4–1, and I was leading the conference in passing yards when we faced off against Washington State on the road. Less than a minute into the second quarter, I stepped into a pass and got caught in a scrum at the line, and then a Washington State linebacker rolled into my right leg. We still won, but I ended up sitting out the next two weeks with a sprained knee. We finished at a modest 7–6, but it was a solid season statistically, with 3,191 total passing yards and twenty touchdowns.

My senior year was memorable for a couple of reasons. We started off terribly, losing five of our first six games and, as a result, Coach Stoops. He was fired midseason, immediately following a tough loss to Oregon State on the road. Tim Kish, our defensive coordinator, took over as interim head coach, and we ended up finishing out the season at a disappointing 4–8. As much as I liked Tim, it was difficult losing Coach Stoops midway through the season. He believed in me when a lot of other people didn't, and I'll always be indebted to him for that.

During that time of leadership turnover, I was particularly grateful for a couple of people on the UA staff: Frank Scelfo and Corey Edmond. Frank was the quarterbacks coach, and without his expertise, I wouldn't have been NFL ready. Corey (aka Coach Ed), the strength coach, was not only a motivator in the weight room; he also showed me what it looks like to be a man of faith and to live that out in the world of football.

Ironically, even though we finished dead last in the conference, it ended up being one of my best seasons ever, statistically speaking. I completed 69 percent of my passes for 4,334 yards and twenty-eight touchdowns—all single-season records for Arizona—and ranked first in the Pac-12 for total offense per game.

As for the girl . . . believe it or not, she dated my roommate sophomore year. While that isn't the way I would have drawn it up, it wasn't so bad. For one thing, it gave me an excuse to spend a lot of time around her. As it turned out, we had a lot in common: we were both athletes, and we both came from tight-knit families. Her older brother Evan was a tight end for the Cleveland Browns, so she knew football. And most important, she was a strong Christian.

Even after Tori and my friend were no longer together, Tori and I remained good friends. I always imagined ending up with someone like her, but we never dated—at least not while we were in college.

That would have been too easy.

Instead, we decided to wait until we lived almost three thousand miles apart.

FEELING A DRAFT

In April, heading into the draft, there was a lot of uncertainty about how things would play out for me. I was coming off a record-setting season, but the pro scouts didn't know what to make of me. I wasn't a player who made everyone say, "Oh, this guy is a first-round lock." It was more of a "Let's see where this guy goes" kind of vibe.

I put up big numbers at Arizona, but I did so for a team that went 19–19 during my time as a starter. And because we were often playing from behind, I was throwing a lot—all of which factored into each team's decision-making process. My mobility was another concern. I've got a strong arm, but I'm pretty much a classic pocket passer. I can move around well, but I'm not going to blow anyone away at a track meet. It's just not my thing, and my performance at the combine confirmed that. It also confirmed something else: I really should have gotten a haircut prior to my skills test.

My hair was really long and shaggy at the time, which normally wasn't a problem, because I always practiced with a hat or a helmet on. But at the combine, we weren't allowed to wear either, so every time I dropped back to throw, my hair kept getting in my face, meaning a large percentage of my passes were basically done blind.

Still, I ended up interviewing with virtually every team, though the Eagles were the only team that gave me an individual workout leading up to the draft. Doug Pederson, who was the Eagles' quarterbacks coach at the time, came out to Austin to put me through the paces in my old stomping grounds at Westlake.

It was an unusually cold and windy day in Austin, and Doug had me throw what's called a divide route, which is basically a long, diagonal route anywhere from 50 to 65 yards down the field. It was the first time I'd ever thrown this route in my career, and naturally,

I was throwing into the wind. I dropped back, cocked my arm, and let it fly. The ball came out wobbly and hit the wind like a wall. It died in mid-air and fluttered to the ground about twenty-five yards out—five yards short of Doug.

Aww, man, I thought. *That's not good.*

I was mortified. Because let's face it: if you're going to play anywhere on the East Coast or up north, you've *got* to be able to throw in weather like that.

As soon as the ball landed, I turned to Doug and said, "I want another one."

He gave me a second shot, and this time I launched it—a perfect, tight spiral that cut through the wind like a knife and hit the receiver in stride fifty yards downfield.

That's what I'm talkin' about.

A few days later, I met privately with head coach Andy Reid and his staff in Philadelphia. I kept telling myself, *There's no way they're going to draft me.* They already had Michael Vick. I wasn't their style—they wanted guys like Mike who were known for using their legs just as much as their arm. Still, I had tremendous respect for Coach Reid, and regardless of whether they were serious about me, I wanted to show him I was serious about them.

"So, Nick," Coach Reid stared me down, "are you ready to play here?"

I honestly had no idea. But I sure wasn't going to tell him that. So with all the courage a brazen twenty-three-year-old NFL hopeful could muster, I sat up straight in my chair and shot back, "Yes, I am."

His eyes narrowed cynically. "You know, this city has torn grown men apart," he said. "This is a tough place to play. You need thick skin, and you need to know who you are, because you're gonna go through the wringer here. I promise you that."

Huh, I thought. *Maybe I'm* not *ready to play in Philadelphia.*

I knew he was right. The Philadelphia media is legendary for being tough on its athletes. But I held my ground.

"I can play here," I assured him. "I know I can."

He just smiled at me and shook his head.

The next morning, I flew back home to Austin and waited for draft day to arrive.

I wasn't invited to New York for the actual event, but that was fine with me, because I honestly had no clue where I'd be drafted—or if I'd get drafted at all. In fact, I was fully prepared to become an undrafted free agent. So I just settled in at my parents' house with my sisters, Lacey and Katie; my grandfather; my parents; and a couple of buddies to watch it all unfold on TV.

In a move that surprised no one, the Colts opened the draft by selecting Andrew Luck with the number one pick. Immediately after that, the Redskins went with Robert Griffin III. A few minutes later, Miami selected Ryan Tannehill. Three quarterbacks were already off the board, and they hadn't even gotten to the tenth pick yet. About an hour later, the Cleveland Browns picked up Brandon Weeden with the twenty-second pick, closing out the first round.

As the draft wore on, two more quarterbacks got picked up— Brock Osweiler went to Denver in the second round (57), followed by Russell Wilson, who went to Seattle in the third (75).

By this point, things were starting to look pretty grim. The Eagles had already selected three defensive players, but they had yet to make their pick in the third round. I reached down and patted the cell phone in my pocket, willing it to ring. Then, just as the Bengals selected Mohamed Sanu, a wide receiver out of Rutgers (83), the power went out.

"Seriously?" I jumped up from the couch. "It isn't even storming."

As everyone started stumbling around in the dark looking for candles and flashlights, I reached down to grab my phone so I could at least follow the next few picks online. That's when I realized it wasn't there.

Shoot. It must have fallen out of my pocket when I got up.

"Hey, guys!" I called out. "Help me find my phone!" I couldn't believe it. I was waiting for the most important call of my life, and I'd lost my phone in the dark.

So there we were, crawling around on our hands and knees in the dark, when Katie called out, "Here it is!"

Don't ask me how, but somehow when my phone fell out of my pocket, it not only landed facedown but switched over to vibrate. Fortunately, Katie was crawling right next to it when it went off. "It's a Philadelphia number!"

Quicker than you can say "Ron Jaworski," I grabbed the phone from her and headed to the porch.

"Hey, Nick." It was the Eagles' general manager, Howie Roseman, and Coach Reid. I froze. Then Andy nonchalantly asked, "Are you okay if we take you with the eighty-eighth pick in a couple minutes?"

I love that guy.

"Yes, sir!"

I'd have been happy if they'd taken me dead last.

My dad saw me on the phone and made his way over to me. "The Eagles are about to draft me," I mouthed to him. "They're taking me with the eighty-eighth pick!"

Back in the house, the celebration had already started. Because the power was still out, I didn't get to see my name being called on TV, but I didn't care.

I had made it.

I was officially in the NFL.

CHAPTER 2

IT'S NOT EASY BEING GREEN

The year before I was drafted by the Eagles, *GQ* magazine ran an article called "The Worst Sports Fans in America," and guess who came in at number one? That's right—Eagles fans. The article was all done in fun, and even the editors acknowledged the complete lack of scientific research supporting their claims, but there's no denying that Eagles fans have a very, well, *colorful* reputation. And that's exactly what I love about them.

Now bear in mind that I grew up in Texas, where football is practically a religion. But Philly fans are a breed unto themselves. If you're an outsider, you've probably heard the wild stories about fans throwing snowballs at Santa and hurling beer bottles and batteries onto the field. But I promise, Philly fans are some of the most loyal, passionate fans in the NFL—solid, hardworking people who love their city and their sports teams.

And almost everyone has a story.

Virtually every Eagles fan I've met has a story about a family member who grew up loving the Eagles. If it's not their parents, it's their grandparents or their great-grandparents. Eagles fandom is generational, and those roots run deep. As far as their fans are concerned, the Eagles *are* family, which, if you think about it, explains a lot. The people who love you most push you harder and expect more of you than anyone else. They know you're capable of accomplishing great things, and they want to see you achieve them. That's tough love. That's the city of Philly.

By the time I arrived in town in May 2012, the Philadelphia faithful had been waiting for a Super Bowl championship for forty-six years. In fact, the last time they'd won *any* league title was when Hall of Fame quarterback Norm "the Dutchman" Van Brocklin led the Eagles to the 1960 NFL championship over Vince Lombardi's Green Bay Packers. In other words, Eagles fans had been waiting a long time for something to celebrate.

As for me, I was just getting started.

LIKE DRINKING FROM A FIRE HOSE

My first few weeks in Philly were a blur. In a lot of ways, it reminded me of my freshman year at Michigan State, only multiplied exponentially. I had to learn a whole new offense and *a lot* of new verbiage, practically overnight.

Because Andy Reid is an offensive genius, our playbook was filled with a bunch of long, complicated plays, like "Shift to gun trips right bunch 74 chip F deep cross halfback check middle." It was like trying to master a foreign language in less than a week, but with people running after you the whole time. Most days it was all I could do to remember what the play was. More often than not, I just dropped back in the pocket, tried to decipher what was going on in front of me, and let it rip.

On top of everything else, I had the blessing and the curse of training alongside Mike Vick, one of the most dynamic players to ever play the game. Man, was I in awe of that guy. He could throw a picture-perfect seventy-five-yard dart off his back foot like it was nothing. Seriously, that guy was unbelievable.

And while I realize every rookie says this, it's true: in the NFL, everything moves unbelievably fast. It's incredibly intimidating, but you can't show fear because all the coaches, coordinators, and assistants are critiquing your every move. If you can't cut it, physically or mentally, there's a long line of guys waiting in the wings who would love to take your spot.

It's an absurd amount of pressure, but it's all part of the rookie experience.

That first week, I was rooming with another rookie. He was a great guy and a talented quarterback out of the University of Miami. The Eagles had signed him as an undrafted free agent about a week after the draft. One day when we were hanging out in our hotel room, the phone rang. It was the personnel department, telling him he had been released. He had to turn in his playbook and equipment, and he had a flight booked to go home. It was pretty brutal.

He had a chance to say some quick good-byes and pack up his things, but he didn't have room for everything. "Listen," he told me, "if any of the hotel staff wants any of my shoes, tell them they can have them."

Like I said, in the NFL, everything happens unbelievably fast.

NOT-SO-BROTHERLY LOVE

One thing that did provide me some sanity during those grueling weeks was chatting with Tori Moore. After being close friends all through college, we would occasionally catch up. Shortly after graduation, I left for Philly, and Tori took a job with Nike in Beaverton, Oregon—2,800 miles away.

The next May, I had to head to LA for a Rookie Premiere event. Knowing that Tori didn't live too far away, I asked her to join me—as a friend. We had chatted about how we hadn't seen each other in a while and how it would be fun to catch up in person, so this wasn't out of the blue. Unfortunately, Tori was going to be out of town at the time. She hinted about getting together in the summer sometime, but that wouldn't happen unless one of us flew across the country. The problem is that it's not really casual or friendly to fly across the country to see a girl. We both wanted this to happen, though, so there was clearly something going on that was more than friendship.

In June, I booked a trip to Portland to see Tori. We both agreed that this might not work out, but we wanted to explore the possibility. Since we weren't sure where the relationship was headed, we decided not to tell anyone about the visit.

Here's where things got complicated—and funny. As I made my way through the airport, trying to head out under the radar, I ran into Trent Edwards (who later became my roommate). Trent was a sixth-year veteran who had just signed a one-year deal with the Eagles. As it happened, he was also a former teammate and close friend of Tori's brother Evan.

I tried to dodge him, but when you're six foot five and 245 pounds, you tend to stand out.

"Hey, Nick," he said, surprised. "Funny seeing you here."

Hysterical.

"Where you headed?"

"Oh, I'm going to LA," I lied. "I have to do another signing."

He looked at the gate listing behind me. "Then why are you at the Portland gate?"

Don't panic.

"Oh . . . well, for some reason, the flight I'm on is going through Portland to LA."

He just stared at me for a second.

Stay cool.

"Huh." He nodded. "That's kind of crazy."

Then, just when I thought I was in the clear, he said, "You know, Tori lives near Portland."

Man, I was this close.

"She does?" I tried my best to sound surprised.

I was starting to feel guilty. Trent was a good guy, and I hated lying to him. But there was no going back now.

"You should see if you can grab lunch together at the airport while you're there," he suggested.

Awesome.

"That's a great idea, Trent. Thanks!"

The only thing that made me feel better than seeing Trent walk away from the departure gate at Philly was seeing Tori pull up to the arrivals doors in Portland.

The second I saw her, I knew.

We had a fantastic weekend. She showed me all around Nike. I told her about the close call with Trent at the airport. We talked. We laughed. This was beyond anything we'd experienced in college.

It almost felt like we'd been dating forever—there was this

chemistry that seemed to develop overnight. In some relationships, the romance starts first and then you really get to know someone. We worked in the opposite order, and that gave us a strong foundation to build on.

That night we went on our first official date. We're both foodies, so I trusted Tori with the dinner selection. She chose a trendy pizza spot in downtown Portland called Oven and Shaker. It wasn't your average first date, where each person orders one thing and neither eats much because of nerves and awkwardness. We went all out. We ordered a couple of appetizers and a salad, which turned out to be the best Caesar salad in Portland at the time. (Hey, that's important to note if you love food.) Following the salad, we ordered a couple of pizzas, including the spicy salami. We ate a ton and kept chatting about how crazy it was that we were sitting in a restaurant in downtown Portland together.

After our first date, we just knew we were going to be something more than friends. Sure, I had to head back to Philly after the weekend was over, and she was focused on starting her career at Nike, but we would figure it out. I knew she was the person I would marry, and I was almost certain she felt the same about me.

A LOT TO PLAY FOR

While my love life may have been trending upward, back in Philadelphia, I was still trying to wrap my head around our new offense—only now I would be doing it live in preseason.

When you're a rookie, you don't get a lot of practice snaps, so the preseason is your first real opportunity to show everyone what you can do. And this preseason in particular carried more meaning than most. The Sunday before our preseason opener against Pittsburgh, Andy Reid lost his twenty-nine-year-old son, Garrett. I can't even begin to imagine what Andy must have been going through that week. How he kept it together on the sideline that night I'll never know. Andy's got a gruff exterior, but underneath he's one of the warmest, most caring people I've ever met. So when I got my chance to play, you'd better believe I gave it everything I had.

Despite the fact that I'd never even seen an NFL game in person before, let alone taken the field in one, I threw two touchdown passes that night—the first a forty-five-yard bomb to Damaris Johnson and the second a forty-four-yard "go" route to Mardy Gilyard. Back-to-back touchdown passes—and they couldn't have come on a better night.

We ended up winning that game on a last-second field goal, and when it was all over, the fans went absolutely berserk, chanting, "Andy! Andy! Andy!" I swear, you'd have thought we'd just won the Super Bowl.

LIKE MIKE

The following week we flew to Foxborough to take on the Patriots. I was expecting to play only two or three series in that game, so I was pretty chill heading into Gillette Stadium. I even had a coffee and a doughnut before the game started. I figured, *I've got time. I'm just gonna watch Mike do his thing for two or three quarters and maybe take a handful of snaps in the fourth.*

Then, on our sixth offensive play of the game, Mike got flushed from the pocket and heaved a desperation pass downfield to DeSean Jackson. A fraction of a second later, Jermaine Cunningham drove his helmet into Mike's side, forcing him to the ground. I could tell almost instantly that Mike was hurt. When he tried to get up, he grabbed his side, grimaced, and fell down again.

As the medical staff rushed onto the field, I scrambled to find my helmet and get in a couple of quick practice throws. It was the first time I'd ever played with our starting lineup, so I wasn't sure what to expect. But when I got to the huddle, the entire line zeroed in on me as if I were Mike. It was a great confidence boost.

I ended up having a pretty good game, going eighteen of twenty-eight for 217 yards. I also added two more touchdowns to my stat sheet. Both were short passes to Clay Harbor—one for three yards and another for one. Not exactly highlight-reel fodder, but hey, I was happy to take what I could get.

Unfortunately, I also threw my first interception. It was my own fault. There were seventeen seconds left in the second quarter, and coverage was tight all over the field. I should have just thrown the ball away, but at the last second I saw Jeremy Maclin waving me down inside the ten, so I heaved it downfield. It ended up getting picked off by Nate Ebner, who ran it all the way back to the thirty-seven before DeSean took him out. Even so, we won the game. And I had shown that I could play with the best of them.

Since Mike was still recovering from his rib injury, they gave me the start in the third preseason game against the Browns. We won that game, and I went twelve of nineteen for two more touchdowns and one interception. I only played one more series in the preseason finale against the Jets, completing four of six passes for forty-six yards, but I'd done enough to earn myself the number two spot behind Mike heading into the regular season. Things were definitely looking up.

Then the season started.

POCKET PRESSURE

We came out of the gate strong, winning three of our first four games. Then we went into a tailspin and lost four in a row, heading into a rivalry game against Dallas at home.

Just when it seemed like things couldn't get worse, we hit a major setback.

In that Dallas game, Mike took two really hard hits early in the second quarter—one in the pocket and another while scrambling for a first down. He got up slowly after the first hit, but because Mike's a warrior, he shook it off and kept playing. After he went down the second time, though, it was clear something was off.

Without even thinking, I grabbed my helmet and started warming up, stopping every couple of throws to check Mike's progress on the sideline. When the training staff took his helmet and started leading him off the field to the locker room, I knew I was up.

I'd played in a handful of preseason games, but this was the real deal—and against Dallas, no less. Needless to say, the butterflies were in full force.

As I continued to warm up, I tried to make a conscious effort to slow my heart rate down, but it wasn't easy. As a backup, you always prepare as if you'll be starting, but even though you might know the game plan inside and out, there's a big difference between playing with the scout team and playing with the starting lineup. So much of a quarterback's success comes down to timing and finding a rhythm with your receivers, and it's hard to establish a rhythm with guys you don't get many practice reps with.

My heart was still racing when I took my first snap. The first pass I threw hit off my receiver's helment, which didn't help me find my stride. After the half, I was finally able to get my nerves under control, and in our first possession of the third quarter, I hit Jeremy Maclin for forty-four yards and a touchdown, putting us up 14–10. For a second there, I actually thought, *Hey, this isn't so bad. I can do this.*

Then I started getting smacked around a little.

On my first play of the fourth quarter, I threw a short pass to the right, intended for LeSean McCoy. It got picked by Anthony Spencer, who returned it for a touchdown. Fortunately, a holding call away from the play brought it back. Talk about catching a break!

But that was the only break I caught that game. On our next drive, on an almost identical play, I threw a short pass to DeSean Jackson that grazed off his fingertips, bounced off a defender, and ricocheted right into the waiting arms of Brandon Carr for a pick six.

With less than a minute to play and the ball on our own one, I got hit from behind trying to scramble out of the end zone. I lost the ball, and the Cowboys recovered it for a touchdown—and the win.

Okay, so maybe this wasn't as easy as I thought.

Since Mike was out with a concussion, I got to start against Washington the following week. I had a less than stellar game, throwing two interceptions and never finding the end zone. We ended up losing 31–6.

With Mike sidelined indefinitely and our season rapidly slipping away, we dropped two more games before heading into Tampa in week fourteen desperate to salvage what was now an abysmal 3–9 record.

Times like these are tough for any team—but this is also when you find out what your team is really made of. It's easy to stay upbeat and maintain your focus when you're winning, but when you haven't posted a win in almost two months, your guys are all banged up, the media is tearing you to shreds, you're tired, you're sore, and nothing is going your way, that's when you either dig deep and battle through it together or pack it up and go home.

We came into Tampa fired up and ready for a fight. And that's exactly what we got. The Bucs' defense completely shut down our running game, and I was facing pressure in the pocket on almost every play. I got sacked twice in a scoreless first quarter, but thanks to an unbelievable receiving performance by Jason Avant, I was able to move us into scoring position right before the half. Andy called a screen pass to the left, and I dropped back and looked to my left. For some reason, the entire defense followed suit, leaving nothing but wide-open space to the right. I've never been much of a sprinter, but when you've picked yourself up off the turf three times in as many series and you catch a glimpse of daylight between you and the post, you tuck that ball down and take off. It might have been the slowest ten-yard touchdown run in history, but I was happy to take it.

That touchdown run, combined with a previous field goal, gave us a 10–0 lead heading into the half. But the Bucs offense came storming back, and we found ourselves down 21–10 with just over seven minutes to play in the fourth.

After marching down the field thanks to some more big plays from Jeremy Maclin, I managed to catch Clay Harbor in the back of the end zone to bring us within five. We missed a two-point conversion attempt, but our defense came through, forced a punt, and got the ball back with just under three minutes to play.

After a rough series that found us facing fourth and five at the twenty-three, with sixteen seconds left on the clock and the pocket breaking down, I hurled a twenty-two-yarder. I hit Jason Avant at the one with ten seconds left to play.

Our offense was gassed, but we hustled it to the line and managed to spike the ball and stop the clock with two seconds left.

Marty Mornhinweg, our offensive coordinator, called a quick-pocket pass play, but after seeing the way the defense was lined up, I didn't like the look of it, so I called a time-out and headed over to the sideline.

Coach Reid waved me over. "What play do you want?"

"I want Q8 sidewinder."

"Okay. Let's do it."

In retrospect, I really have to hand it to Coach Reid. There we were, with our season tanking, a yard away from our first victory in two months, and he let his rookie quarterback make the final call. You've gotta love that.

I went back to the huddle, called a sprint pass to the right, and stepped up to the line. As soon as I got the ball, I rolled out to the right, saw Jeremy in the end zone, and fired it low and to the pylon. Jeremy went to his knees, made the catch, and then skidded out of bounds just as the clock ticked down to 0:00. This put the final score at 23–21, giving me my first career win and ending our eight-game losing streak.

By most accounts, that was a meaningless game, but it meant the world to us. We struggled and fell behind, but we stuck together, gutted it out, and finished strong. And that's what great teams do.

Let me tell you, though, I took a real beating that game—*six* sacks. My whole body was throbbing. After the game, I just sat at my locker, thinking, *Man, if this is what it takes to win a game in this league, I'm not sure how many I've got in me.*

No matter. At least I had one I'd be able to tell my kids about someday.

TOUGH BREAK

My rookie season ended with a whimper—or, more accurately, a fracture.

In the second to last game of the season (a 27–20 loss at home to the Redskins), I suffered a broken right hand—my throwing hand—near the base of my index finger. The funny thing is, I'm not even sure how or when it happened. I remember the pocket breaking down at one point in the first half and then scrambling forward for some yards. But to be honest, I had so much adrenaline flowing through me, I didn't even notice anything was wrong until the game was over.

My injury didn't require surgery, but it was still season ending.

By that point Mike was fully recovered and was able to start the final game against the Giants, which we lost 42–7. We finished the season with a record of 4–12. It was a terrible year marked by a lot of tough losses—and one of the worst was yet to come.

The next day, the Eagles fired Coach Reid. Even though he was the winningest coach in franchise history and one of the longest-tenured head coaches in the league (fourteen years), the writing had been on the wall for several weeks.

Andy's firing was especially difficult for me. He was the first guy in the NFL who really believed in me. He gave me a chance when nobody else would, he saw things in me that even I didn't know were there, and he pushed me to do more than I ever thought possible. And when the chips were down and the game was on the line, he trusted me to lead his team.

In a way, I blamed myself. There's always a chance that if a young quarterback can come in and win a couple of games at the end of the season, the coach will get another chance. I'd hoped that I could spark a turnaround and repay Andy for everything he'd done for me. But sadly, it just wasn't meant to be.

GROWTH MENTALITY

In many respects, my rookie season was a lot like my final year at Arizona. We had a terrible season, finished dead last in the conference, and lost our head coach. I didn't have as solid of a year statistically as I'd had at Arizona, but I did get my first career start and my first career win. I also managed to master the Reid offense and threw for 1,700 yards. Not a bad start, considering how my predraft workout began.

On a personal level, things were starting to get serious with Tori. Our schedules had kept us both pretty busy throughout the regular season, but we talked and Skyped constantly, and now that I would have a little time off, I was really looking forward to seeing her again.

I had also grown a lot spiritually since my early days in Arizona, thanks in large part to my teammate Jason Avant and our chaplain, Theodore Winsley. In addition to being a spectacular wide receiver, Jason is a force on the basketball court and one of the most solid Christians I've ever met. We met in training camp, but the subject of faith didn't come up at first.

Then, after our second preseason game against the Patriots, Jason grabbed me by the jersey and pulled me aside. I figured he was going to talk to me about a passing route or something, but instead he said, "Hey, Nick, I just wanted you to know I've been praying for you all week, because I feel like something big is about to happen to you."

It meant a lot to know he was praying for me. From that point on, we started spending more time together.

Every week during that season, Jason and I would go to the Bible study Pastor Ted led. After a while, a bond formed between our group of guys that I truly believe made us stronger as a team, especially when things got tough—which, in 2012, was often. There's something about having a group of guys out there praying for you, supporting you, encouraging you, and keeping you grounded that makes even the worst of times feel more manageable.

It was a good thing we had something to build on, because as trying as that 2012 season was, 2013 would be even harder.

CHAPTER 3

CHIPPING AWAY

The firing of Andy Reid hit me hard. But I knew by now how quickly life moves in the NFL. If you can't adapt, you won't survive.

When the Eagles replaced Coach Reid with Chip Kelly in January 2013, I wasn't sure how it would affect my status with the team. Would I get a chance to compete with Mike for the number one spot? Would I start the year as a backup again? Would I be traded? I had no idea.

Chip was coming from the University of Oregon, where he had implemented a lightning-quick, no-huddle offense to great success, leading the Ducks to three Pac-12 conference titles and the 2011 BCS national championship game. His teams were good—and they were *fast*.

I'd played against Chip's Ducks three times when I was at Arizona, and I remember looking across the field, wondering, *What in the world are they doing over there? How are they going so fast?*

I was about to find out.

One thing I did know was that Chip always used a dual-threat, zone-read quarterback at Oregon, and I couldn't help thinking, *Wow, that style of play is right in Mike's wheelhouse.* Mike has a great arm, but he poses another threat too—that he'll take off and run for fifteen or twenty yards. Now when there was a 285-pound linebacker closing in, I could get away and pick up some yardage, but it sure wasn't my strong suit. And in a Chip Kelly offense, that definitely gave Mike the edge.

Yeah, I thought, *this might be the end of my time in Philly.*

Once I met Chip, though, he alleviated my concerns. He told me he definitely wanted me in Philly. He said he'd noticed me in college and he liked my competitiveness and my ability to keep getting up after taking a hit. I was starting to see a theme emerging. My coaches might not have known what to make of me, but they respected my resilience. Still, as we headed into training camp that summer, I was hoping to impress Chip with other skills—besides being a very durable punching bag.

After weeks of worrying about whether I'd fit into Chip's system, once we got started, I absolutely fell in love with it. Everything about it—setting a fast pace, moving up and down the field, and keeping the defense off balance—was just awesome. It reminded me a lot of fast-break basketball. I'd always been more explosive on the court than I was on the field, but this offense really narrowed the gap. Being forced to read and react at a rapid pace played to strengths that had been dormant for a while.

Anytime you have an opportunity to play in a different scheme, you learn more not only about the game but also about yourself. Most players aren't fortunate enough to play in the same offense their whole career. They get traded to another team or their coach goes somewhere else. So if you only know one type of offense—even if you're excellent at it—you'll never become versatile enough to succeed in the NFL. Resilience is about more than just being able to take a hit. It's about being able to adapt on the fly, learning new ways of doing things, and not just surviving but thriving in an ever-changing environment. Change is inevitable. How you react to it is up to you.

One thing was for sure: Chip's offense was all about reaction. It was very simple in theory, yet complicated to execute. Basically, it boiled down to attention to detail. We needed to be able to scan the field and identify schemes and coverages quickly and then adapt accordingly—and immediately. In other words, we had to know the scheme but play by instinct.

We still had a full playbook, but instead of getting the play radioed to me and then communicating everything in the huddle, there was a whole team of signal callers on the sidelines. The linemen and receivers had a signal caller and so did the running back, and we had a couple of dummy signalers so the opposing team couldn't key in on the plays. My instructions came from Chip through my headset. It was the same info, just a lot faster. It's quite a brilliant system, actually.

It wasn't just the in-game concepts that were new. Chip also introduced a whole new way of thinking about Monday through Saturday. Chip had a game plan for everything—the way practice was set up, the speed we practiced at, the recovery methods we used, what we did in the weight room, our pregame routines, the protein shake stations he was famous for, the special stretching routines we did after practice. And it really paid off. Even though we were playing at a faster tempo, we weren't getting fatigued. In fact, we were actually feeling stronger.

A lot of that had to do with Chip's focus on sports science.

Back in 2013, things like sports science and GPS tracking were already big in professional soccer, but they hadn't really taken hold in the NFL yet. In fact, to my knowledge, Chip was one of the first head coaches in the league to fully implement the technology and methodology of advanced sports science into his training regimen. And believe me, it was intense.

It all started during the off-season, while we were still making the mental shift from Coach Reid's West Coast–style offense to Chip's no-huddle system. Chip brought in some new strength coaches and sports-science staff, and every morning during training camp we'd have to weigh in, pee in a cup to check our hydration levels, get our heart rate monitored, and fill out a questionnaire about how much sleep we'd gotten and how sore we were. It might sound like overkill, but the science is sound, and there's no question that our team benefited.

Heading into our first preseason game against the Patriots, I was feeling stronger and healthier than ever. So was Mike. That week Chip announced that Mike and I would be competing for the starting position.

Then, just as the competition was starting to heat up, I got blindsided with a setback.

UNEXPECTED HIT

While I was in Philly fighting for a starting position, out in Oregon Tori was facing her own battle. A few weeks earlier, she had been at an outdoor picnic concert hanging out with some girlfriends when she suddenly started feeling light-headed. When her symptoms worsened to the point that she started missing work, she decided to see a doctor.

Because she presented with no fever, and her symptoms (dizziness, nausea, fatigue, and some insomnia) were largely invisible, the doctor diagnosed her with depression. That didn't sit well with Tori, so she decided to see another doctor. He said the same thing. So did the next doctor. And the one after that.

By this time Tori was really starting to get frustrated.

"I don't think this is the right diagnosis, Nick." She was close to tears when she called me. "I know something's wrong. I was a college athlete. I know my body. But nobody will listen to me."

I felt so helpless. I agreed that Tori wasn't depressed. She was one of the most upbeat, confident women I'd ever met. But clearly *something* was going on. She felt sick all the time. The week before, she had been running four to five miles a day, but now she was barely able to make it to work. She was having heart palpitations and blinding headaches, and she couldn't keep anything down. Talk about irony—there I was, in peak physical condition yet getting a full battery of medical tests every day, while my girlfriend was struggling just to stand up without feeling faint. And since she looked fine, she couldn't even convince anyone she was sick.

All I wanted to do was jump on the next plane to Portland, hold Tori in my arms, and tell her everything was going to be okay—and possibly give the doctors a piece of my mind. But that was the last thing Tori wanted me to do. She knew this was a huge month for me, and she didn't want anything to distract me. I had a job to do.

Actually, I had a job to *earn*.

LET THE GAMES BEGIN

Despite losing our preseason opener to New England 31–22, Mike and I both played well. Mike threw a perfect forty-seven-yard touchdown pass to DeSean Jackson on his opening drive. I came in at the end of the first quarter, and on my first series, I was driven into the ground by two defensive tackles and lost the ball. But I managed to bounce back and lead a ten-play, sixty-six-yard scoring drive—all in true Chip Kelly fashion, with no huddle.

The following week I started against Carolina, and for the second week in a row, I got off to a rough start. After leading an eleven-play, eighty-seven-yard drive that started back on our own five, we went into the shotgun, and I fumbled the snap. I quickly picked it back up and tried to throw the ball out of the back of the end zone, but I didn't get enough height on it, and it ended up getting picked for a touchback.

If Chip kept me at Philly because of my resilience, I was getting a chance to prove myself in that arena. Once again, I bounced back in the following series. After leading a thirty-two-yard drive down inside the ten, I saw an opening and scrambled seven yards for a touchdown, beating the linebacker to the pylon by about half a step.

The second quarter belonged to Mike, and he was on fire. He started off perfectly—nine for nine and 105 yards. Then, just before the end of the second quarter, he lobbed a desperation pass that got picked off just as time expired.

After the two preseason games, I ended up eleven of fourteen for ninety-six yards, with a rushing touchdown, an interception, and a lost fumble. Mike completed thirteen of fifteen for 199 yards, with a touchdown and an interception. We both played well, but in terms of sheer passing yardage, Mike had the clear edge.

The Tuesday after the Carolina game, Chip officially named Mike the starter for the season. I was disappointed, but Chip made it clear both to me and to the media that it was an extremely close call and that he was pleased with how I'd played.

As for Mike, he couldn't have been more gracious. We were both fierce competitors, but we were also teammates and good friends. Whenever I made a bad play or had a rough series, Mike was always the first one to meet me on the sidelines, offering encouragement and support—and I did the same for him. Competition aside, I knew Mike would always have my back, and he knew I'd always have his.

That relationship would prove especially important heading into the season. No matter your offense, the NFL is grueling. You have to be ready to play at any moment, because the starter could be just one hit away from leaving the game.

FALSE START

We opened the regular season with a big Monday night win over the Redskins at FedEx Field. Mike had a great game, going fifteen of twenty-five for 203 yards, scoring two touchdowns through the air and running for a third. But the real star of the evening was Chip Kelly's offense. Our up-tempo, no-huddle approach caught Washington completely off guard. By the fourth quarter, the entire defensive line was totally gassed, people were cramping up, and all along the Washington sideline, guys were sucking on oxygen masks.

And the Philadelphia faithful loved it. Fans who had been skeptical at the end of our rather lackluster 2–2 preseason were suddenly saying, "Hey, this Chip Kelly thing is pretty cool."

Then we lost our next three games.

In week five, we traveled to MetLife Stadium to take on the 0–4 Giants. Late in the second quarter, after rushing for seventy-nine yards, Mike pulled up out of bounds after a thirteen-yard broken play scramble. He grimaced and grabbed the back of his left hamstring.

As we watched the play in slow motion up on the Jumbotron, discouraged choruses of "It's a hammy" traveled up and down the Eagles' sideline. He continued to play through that series, but it quickly became clear that he wouldn't be able to make it through the game. It was now my turn to lead the Kelly juggernaut.

As Mike gingerly made his way over to the bench to be checked out, I said a quick prayer that he'd be okay, grabbed my helmet, and headed onto the field.

I started off slow, but in the fourth quarter, our defense came up strong, forcing three turnovers, which allowed me to throw for two touchdowns, putting us up 36–21 and ending our three-game losing streak.

With Mike's hamstring still on the mend, I started the next game at Tampa and had the best game of my career to date, completing 71 percent of my passes for 296 yards and three touchdowns in a 31–20 win—a performance that earned me my first NFC offensive player of the week award.

Then, just when everything seemed to be turning around, the Cowboys came to town. For whatever reason, their man coverage gave us fits, and we were unable to do anything on offense, going scoreless for the first half. Then, in the final seconds of the third quarter, down 10–0 and desperate to get something going, I started to scramble on third and goal and got absolutely plastered by George Selvie and Jarius Wynn. When I went down, my head snapped back and my helmet hit the ground so hard I felt dizzy. As I sat up and attempted to shake off the cobwebs, the first thought that ran through my mind was, *Man, I should have just thrown it away.* I can't remember what my second thought was. The next thing I knew, I was being led over to the bench by Chris Peduzzi, our head athletic trainer, to be evaluated for a concussion.

"Hold your head still and follow my finger," Chris said. "How are you feeling?"

"I'm not sure," I managed. Everything was spinning a bit.

"Can you tell me what day it is?"

I paused for a second. "Sunday." That seemed to make sense. *Why else would we be playing? Unless it's Monday.*

"Do you know what quarter it is?"

I tried to focus. "It's the third—no, the fourth."

"Can you tell me what happened?"

I couldn't remember the specific play, but I definitely remembered how it ended.

"I got hit."

Chris mumbled something to the trainer standing next to him and then took my helmet away. "That's it, Nick," he said. "You're done for the day." Then he led me back to the locker room.

As we walked, he rattled off a list of three or four words and told me to remember them. A few minutes later, he asked me to repeat them. I think I got one or two of them right, but I wouldn't bet on it.

After a few more questions, the gist of which I can't remember, they took me back to the training room for a more thorough examination. The examination confirmed what Chris suspected and I dreaded: I had a concussion.

It would be two weeks before I saw the field again.

SILVER LINING

The days immediately following the Dallas game were a blur. I had a constant, low-grade headache and was having a hard time concentrating. Even the smallest amount of light made my eyes pound so hard I thought they were going to explode.

Every morning I'd go in for treatment, then head back to my apartment to rest behind blackout curtains for the rest of the day. I didn't attend any team meetings or practices, and when we hosted the Giants the following week, I wasn't even able to go to the game.

The one silver lining of an otherwise miserable week was that my mom and Tori had both flown to Philadelphia to help me recuperate. It was the first time I'd seen Tori in months, but as wonderful as it was to be together, it was hard to see what a toll her illness had taken on her.

The good news was that she finally had a name for what was making her sick. After seeing multiple doctors, she finally saw a neurologist. The doctor ran a test that measured her heart rate and blood pressure, first when she was lying down and then when she was standing. The test revealed that her heart rate increased by more than thirty beats per minute when she changed position. No wonder she was nauseous, dizzy, and exhausted and had trouble standing for more than a few minutes.

The neurologist's diagnosis was postural orthostatic tachycardia syndrome, or POTS, which is essentially a dysfunction in the autonomic nervous system. The autonomic nervous system controls all the functions of the body that should happen automatically, such as blood pressure, heart rate, breathing, and digestion. When these functions are disrupted, they require careful management. Tori had to constantly monitor how she felt, drink lots of fluids, and increase her sodium intake to keep everything stable. It was a relief to have a diagnosis, but we had no idea how long the road ahead would be.

Beyond the struggle of the symptoms themselves, it was hard to deal with a condition that is often misdiagnosed and misunderstood. There is currently no cure, and most of the treatment options are still in the experimental stage. Even with medication, her symptoms escalated to the point that she had to leave her job at Nike and move back home with her parents in Wisconsin. It pained her to give up that job, but it was just too much for her to continue living by herself when she needed to focus on getting healthy again.

She put on a brave face when she was in Philly, but I could tell she was struggling. As miserable as I felt, she'd been dealing with even worse symptoms—and for a whole lot longer. Still, I was grateful to have her close by. I was glad neither of us had to deal with these health setbacks alone.

SEVENTH HEAVEN

By week nine, I had passed all the concussion protocols and had gotten the starting nod for our game at Oakland. The team was really struggling. Mike had started the week eight game against the Giants and reinjured his hamstring, giving way to rookie Matt Barkley. Matt played hard, and despite having limited practice reps, he went seventeen of twenty-six for 158 yards. Our defense managed to capitalize on an errant snap that sailed over Steve Weatherford's head late in the fourth quarter, but we still lost the game 15–7.

Going into Oakland, we were sitting at 3–5, and our offense hadn't scored a touchdown since facing Tampa in week six. Even though I was feeling better physically, I was struggling emotionally and spiritually. It had been a tough season—not just in terms of adjusting to a new coach and learning a new offense, but also in terms of dealing with the separation from Tori during such a difficult time in her life.

When you're a quarterback, everyone on the field looks to you for leadership. You're the guy calling the shots. You're the one in control. But at that point, I didn't feel like I had control over anything. I couldn't fix Tori's health problems, and to be perfectly honest, I wasn't entirely convinced I could fix our offense. I felt like I had to make everyone proud and accomplish great things, but I didn't know how. I was supposed to be the guy everyone looked to for answers, but at that moment, all I had were questions.

Why can't we make this offense work?

What if I'm part of the problem?

What if I let everyone down?

Should I be playing or taking care of Tori?

Is this even what I'm supposed to be doing with my life?

This is all I've ever done. If I'm not a football player anymore, who am I?

Not exactly your typical pregame self-talk.

That afternoon before the game, while most of the guys were blasting their music and pumping themselves up, I was off by my locker, praying. *God, I don't know if this is what I'm supposed to be doing. If it's your will for me to keep playing this game, please help me to see that. And if it's not, please give me the wisdom and the courage to do what you want me to do.*

I know God doesn't always provide visible signs in response to our prayers. In fact, most of the time we just have to walk in faith and trust that he will show us each next step. In many respects, the game against Oakland was my step of faith. And boy, did God show up.

From the second we stepped onto the field, everything clicked. My first touchdown pass was a two-yard crossing route to tight end Brent Celek in the closing minutes of the first quarter. After that, the touchdowns started piling up.

I hooked up with Riley Cooper twice in the second quarter—once for seventeen and once for sixty-three. Then I hit Zach Ertz in the back of the end zone on a fifteen-yard scramble to the right, putting us up 28–13 at the half.

On our opening drive of the second half, I threw a wide route to the right and hit a wide-open LeSean McCoy, who ran twenty-five yards—untouched—into the end zone. And the hits just kept coming. On our next possession, I tossed a forty-six-yarder to DeSean Jackson, who leaped into the end zone, putting us up 42–13. By the time I threw my final scoring pass late in the third quarter—a five-yard toss, again to Riley—all I could think was, *Man, this is unreal.*

When the clock ran out, I'd completed twenty-two of twenty-eight passes for 406 yards and seven touchdowns—the latter mark tying an NFL record held by the likes of Peyton Manning, as well as Hall of Famers George Blanda, Sid Luckman, and Y. A. Tittle.

By the end of the game, I was more stunned than anyone by all that had transpired.

IN THE ZONE

Professional athletes—whether in the NFL or otherwise—often talk about being "in the zone" or how the game "slows down." It's a strange phenomenon, and it's a little difficult to describe. But it's a real thing. And when it happens, it's pretty cool.

Maybe the best way to explain it is by describing what it's *not.* When the game moves too fast, it's the equivalent of having one of those days when everything falls apart. Your body is stressed and tight, and you're battling one negative thought after another. All you want to do is to pack it up, go to bed, and hope that tomorrow is better.

When the game moves too fast, it could be because the defense is showing you a look you didn't prepare for or because you've been knocked down one too many times. Maybe you threw an interception that's still eating at you, you bobbled an early snap, or you got a couple of passes batted down at the line. Whatever it is, something has you rattled, and you're filled with just enough fear and doubt to be out of whack.

That's when you start overthinking everything that's going on. Instead of using your senses to assess the situation, your mind starts playing tricks on you. You start seeing things. You might be looking at the defense head-on, but your mind is making stuff up. *Which way are they bringing the blitz? Are they even going to blitz, or are they bluffing? What coverage are they playing with this safety rotation?* In quarterback speak, it's called "seeing ghosts," and every quarterback faces it at some point in the season.

On the flip side, when you're in the zone and everything slows down, it's almost as if you're not even thinking—you're just reacting. It's all instinct. Your heart rate slows down, your breathing is calm, and you see everything clearly. Chip used to tell me, "Don't overthink. Just grip it and rip it." That's what it means to be in the zone.

In a way, being in the zone is kind of the football equivalent of trusting God. Instead of overthinking everything or trying to take everything on yourself, you turn it over to God and let him carry the weight. You do your part, and then you trust God to do the rest. You get through the hard times by leaning on God to sustain you. That's the amazing thing about faith: when you're at your weakest, that's when God shows his strength.

After the game, I remember sitting by my locker, thinking, *Wow, I just did something that shouldn't have even been possible.*

This was a game both my team and I could build on.

ICING ON THE CAKE

That Oakland game was a turning point in my career. Catapulted by that performance, I remained the starter for the rest of the year. In fact, after our week thirteen win over Arizona, Chip told reporters that I was going to be his starting quarterback "for the next thousand years."

I ended up finishing the regular season with twenty-seven touchdowns and two interceptions—the best ratio in NFL history—and a league-leading 119.2 passer rating. Even better, we won six of our final seven games, clinching the NFC East division title and officially stamping our ticket to the playoffs. Not a bad turnaround for a team that had finished 4–12 the previous season.

Given that my first NFL start came against my hometown team, it seemed fitting that I would start my first NFL playoff game against a guy I'd looked up to all through high school: Drew Brees.

Naturally, the media made a huge deal of the fact that Drew and I had gone to the same high school, and truth be told, I was flattered by the comparisons. Not only is Drew a fantastic player who performs at a top level, but he's also a great role model. In fact, that's why I chose Drew's jersey number (9) when I went to Philadelphia. And even though we were never on the field at the same time, it was still pretty cool to stand on the sidelines and watch him in action—at least, as cool as it can be when he's playing against your team.

It was a close game from the start, with both offenses struggling to get things going. We went into halftime leading 7–6 after I hit Riley Cooper on a ten-yard pass late in the second.

We were trailing by six late in the fourth when I found Zach Ertz underneath for a three-yard touchdown, putting us up by one with 4:58 left. That's way too much time to leave for a guy like Drew. The

Saints started with great field position after Darren Sproles reeled off a thirty-nine-yard kickoff return, topped off by a fifteen-yard horse-collar penalty. It was the only possible play to make, and the penalty stopped Darren from taking it all the way down for a touchdown. Then Drew milked the clock with a ten-play possession, setting Shayne Graham up for a thirty-two-yard field goal as time expired. We lost 26–24.

But my season wasn't over yet. I still had one more game to play—this time in Hawaii, at my first Pro Bowl. Getting to play alongside dozens of future Hall of Famers was an experience I'll never forget.

I got to share quarterbacking duties with Cam Newton and Andrew Luck, and I ended up going seven of ten for eighty-nine yards and a touchdown. To top it off, even though I was only an alternate, I was awarded the Pro Bowl offensive MVP award. It was a pretty cool ending to a season that had an incredibly difficult beginning.

The only thing that would have made it even sweeter was if Tori had been able to be there with me. Unfortunately, she was still really struggling with her health, and her condition made flying nearly impossible. As I stood on my hotel balcony watching the sun set over the Hawaiian surf and thanking God for all the miracles in my life, I came to a realization—I didn't want to spend one more day without Tori by my side.

Now I just had to figure out one thing: How should I pop the question?

CHAPTER 4

BLINDSIDED

By February 2014, Tori's health had taken a turn for the worse, and none of the doctors had any real solutions for resolving her symptoms. She was now spending most of each day on the couch and had difficulty just moving around. We decided it was time to take more drastic action, so we headed to Mayo Clinic in Scottsdale. My dad's best friend and business partner, Guy Villavaso (a.k.a. Uncle Guy), had a casita on the grounds of his home just outside of Scottsdale, and he let us stay there while Tori underwent treatment with Dr. Brent Goodman, one of the country's leading POTS specialists.

Neither Tori nor I felt at peace about living together before we were married, but given the severity of her illness, I just couldn't bring myself to leave her alone—especially since her condition made her dizzy and unstable, leaving her at risk to pass out at any moment.

On the heels of a rough couple of weeks full of tests and treatment, we both desperately needed a win. After consulting with Tori's mom, I decided that this was the moment to pop the question. I arranged for our immediate families to fly in so I could surprise Tori with an engagement ring.

To throw her off the scent, I told her that her parents were coming into town to meet with Dr. Goodman and hear about the treatment options. My plan was to pretend we were meeting her parents in town for lunch, then propose to her in front of Uncle Guy's pool while my parents, her parents, and her brothers and their wives all secretly watched and recorded the big moment. The problem was, it didn't make sense to walk past the pool to exit the property, so if I was going to pull this off, I was going to have to come up with something super clever.

Unfortunately, I was also super nervous. After all, this was the biggest moment of my life—bigger than the draft weekend, the playoffs, and the Pro Bowl combined. Tori was the most beautiful and amazing woman I'd ever known, and she had been through so much in the past year. I wanted to make the whole experience extra special for her. As we got ready to leave, I opened my mouth to say something memorable and poetic, but I was such a wreck, all I could manage was, "Hey, why don't we walk down this path to the pool?"

Smooth.

Tori looked down the path and then back at me. "Why would we walk that way? That makes zero sense." Tori wasn't afraid to speak her mind.

"No," I urged. "Let's go over here."

"Nick, come on," she protested, heading toward the main house and our eventual exit.

"Tori, I *really* want to go down by the pool."

At that point she looked at me like I had just announced I would be playing my next NFL game in an adult onesie. My amazing (though clearly not thought-out) plan was backfiring on me big-time. I had to improvise—and fast.

Enter Uncle Guy's beloved dachshund.

"Tori," I pleaded, "you have to come with me. Sammy took a *huge* poop down near the pool."

Really, Nick? Dog poop? That's what you're going with here?

"Seriously, you would not believe the size of the poop that came out of this dog. You have to see it."

Apparently so.

I think it's important to note here that when facing high-pressure situations, professional quarterbacks are expected to respond with a calm, cool demeanor and exhibit an air of confidence that telegraphs to the rest of the team, *Don't worry, guys. I've got this. Just follow me.* Yet there I was, totally freaked out, attempting to lure my future fiancée to our proposal site with the promise of a pile of canine excrement—because apparently, that's what panicky, love-struck idiots do.

The incredible thing is, it worked. Sort of.

"Why would we need to look at that?" Tori sighed. "This better be good."

Despite having dodged a massive bullet, my heart was still pounding. The moment of truth had arrived. Once we finally reached the pool—and without a doggy blessing in sight—I dropped to one knee. I had rehearsed a special speech, but as soon as my knee hit the pavestone, my mind went blank. All I could do was pull out the ring and, with my hands shaking, stammer, "Tori, will you marry me?"

She just stared at me, not saying a word.

Oh, boy. What's happening?

At that moment, all our family members came out of hiding,

applauding. Tori looked at them and back at me. Then she started to cry.

But I still didn't have an answer.

"So . . . is that a yes?" I asked nervously.

"Yes!" she replied through tears. Then she leaned in and kissed me. *Smooth.*

After exchanging congratulatory hugs and handshakes with our families, we all went out for a quick celebratory lunch at the Hopdoddy Burger Bar. Then we changed into our workout gear and headed over to Mayo for Tori's next round of blood tests.

Sammy's excrement, burgers, and blood work. If that's not a fairy-tale engagement story, I don't know what is.

IF YOU THOUGHT THE ENGAGEMENT WAS FANCY . . .

After Tori finished her treatment at Mayo, we moved into a small rental house right across the street from Tori's brother Evan and his wife in Corona Del Mar, a charming little beach town in south Orange County. We still hadn't set a wedding date because of Tori's health, and even though the idea of living together continued to gnaw at us, it didn't make sense for us to live in separate places when she needed so much help.

One weekend in early April, I was sitting outside chatting with my friend Jon Demeter. Jon and I had met at the University of Arizona when he was on staff with Athletes in Action. Along with my strength coach, Coach Ed, who hosted Bible study at his house every Thursday for the players, Jon was one of my first Christian mentors.

Tori was inside with a nurse undergoing an experimental intra-venous immunoglobulin (IVIG) treatment. The doctors thought that if there was an autoimmune issue causing her POTS, this would help to make her less symptomatic. IVIG is a grueling process that takes four, sometimes five, hours over the course of five days, so Jon had stopped by to keep me company while Tori tried to sleep her way through it.

In the middle of our conversation, Jon suddenly switched tracks. "Nick, I feel like I have to call you out on something." He paused for a second before continuing. "You and Tori really shouldn't be living together."

I didn't respond, but inside, I was fuming. *Are you serious? Tori can barely move. As we speak, she's undergoing a five-hour medical treatment, and you're getting on me about this? What do you want me to do, abandon her?*

He just looked at me. "You know I'm right, Nick."

Of course I knew it. Tori and I both knew it. We'd been justifying our decision for months now, but deep down, we both knew what we were doing wasn't in line with what we believed and what the Bible teaches.

"I know," I finally confessed. "I just can't imagine not being with her all the time while she's going through this. Her parents don't live here, and she can't live by herself."

He thought for a moment, then asked, "Have you set a date yet?"

I shook my head. "No. I want Tori to have a big, beautiful wedding—the kind every little girl dreams of. But she's still so weak, I don't think she could even make it down the aisle."

He looked at the house. "Well, what if you just went to the local courthouse and did it there? You could still do a big church wedding later, when Tori's feeling better. But at least this way you'd be honoring God."

"I hadn't even thought of that." I had to admit, it made sense. The question was, what would Tori think?

As soon as Jon left, I went inside to run the idea past her. I honestly had no idea how she would react. I also had no idea that she'd been eavesdropping on our entire conversation.

"Tori," I said, trying to sound as casual as possible. "Jon and I were talking, and—"

"Let's do it," she blurted out.

"What?"

"I heard everything," she said. "I agree 100 percent with everything Jon said."

Whoa. I wasn't expecting that.

"It's something we've both struggled with." She shrugged. "So let's just do it. Let's go down to the courthouse first thing next week and get married."

I just stared at her for a minute.

"It doesn't have to be some huge, elaborate event," she went on. "Sure, that would be nice, but that's not our reality right now. The most important thing is you and me, and both of us honoring God with our relationship."

I love that girl. After all she'd been through, she knew what was really important. Everything had been put into perspective, and we knew this was about more than a fancy wedding.

Tori's parents happened to be in town for the birth of her niece—their first grandchild—and I was glad she could have some family present for the ceremony. Unfortunately, because it was such short notice, there was no way my parents would be able to make it. They felt terrible, but I assured them we both understood. After all, everything was insanely last-minute. The big church wedding was still to come, and they'd be part of our big day.

That should have been enough excitement for one weekend, but we ended up with some medical drama in the mix too. The doctor had warned us that a small percentage of POTS patients who receive IVIG come down with aseptic meningitis, a reaction where the brain swells, resulting in the most unbearable headache you can imagine. On Saturday night, Tori went to bed with what felt like a severe headache, and by midnight it had escalated big-time. After several hours of trying to manage the vomiting and pain at home, things got worse, and we headed to the hospital. Tori spent the rest of the day getting pumped with fluids and pain medication. To our relief, she was able to come home on Sunday night.

Since the ceremony was now less than two days away, I asked her if she wanted to postpone, but she said no. Her parents had already arranged for an attorney friend of theirs who lived in the area to perform the ceremony, and her mother had bought her a dress. And we had already written our vows. Come Wednesday morning, we would be putting those vows into practice—in sickness and in health.

Two days later, Tori and I found ourselves standing in the law offices of Richard C. Watts. Correction: we were sitting. Tori was still too weak to stand for more than a few minutes, so we both stayed seated through the ceremony. But she looked beautiful. Honestly, you never would have guessed that just forty-eight hours earlier she'd been lying in a hospital bed, hooked up to an IV drip and serious pain medication.

The dress her mother had bought for her was simple but beautiful. It wasn't a formal wedding gown—just a pretty white lace dress. Richard even brought a little bouquet of flowers for Tori, a boutonniere for me, and a tiny wedding cake for us both.

The only thing we didn't have yet were wedding bands. But to be perfectly honest, after everything we'd been through over the past several months, we didn't need gold bands to demonstrate our love and commitment to one another, nor did we need an elaborate ceremony. This wouldn't have been our first choice for what our wedding would look like, but it was beautiful in its own way, and we both knew we would cherish it forever. As far as I was concerned, everything I needed was sitting right next to me in a white lace dress.

By the time training camp rolled around, Tori's health had improved significantly. She was still experiencing a few symptoms, but they were more manageable. She began to exercise again, and she was less fatigued. Although she still had to be very calculated about how much energy she used, she was basically a new woman compared to our wedding day.

Later that summer we settled into a little condo on the waterfront in downtown Philadelphia. It was great finally having Tori with me in Philly. Just being able to see her every day and having her there when I got home from practice at night was an answer to prayer.

We were happy in Philly and looking forward to the next season, and I was excited to be filling the slot of starting quarterback. I figured I'd be in Philly for years to come.

FRACTURED SEASON

I was confident heading into the 2014 season, but I also felt a lot more pressure. Since my performance in the Oakland game the previous season, my stock had risen considerably. I'd received endorsement deals from everyone from Bose headphones to Microsoft Surface. It was a wild experience—filming commercials, doing ad campaigns, and seeing myself on billboards—but ultimately, I was in this for the football, not the marketing. All I wanted to do was play football. Plus, whether it was real or perceived, I felt like everyone was holding me to the same twenty-seven-touchdown/two-interception standard I'd set in 2013. Anything less than that would be considered a failure.

That pressure manifested itself in our opening game against Jacksonville, when I fumbled twice and threw an interception less than twenty minutes into the game—just one shy of my 2013 season total in turnovers and putting us down 17–0 at the half. I found my rhythm in the second half, though, and completed two touchdown passes, one of which—a sixty-eight-yarder to Jeremy Maclin—was the longest of my career. We scored thirty-four unanswered points in the second half, making it look like we had two totally different offenses, led by two totally different quarterbacks.

The same thing happened the following week against the Colts. We were down 20–6 in the third, but then we rallied in the fourth to win it 30–27. Two shaky starts, both individually and as a team, but two equally strong finishes. And in football, it's the way you finish that counts.

It was our week three game against Washington that really defined our offense that season. It was a tight, physical game all the way up to the fourth quarter. Then I overthrew Brent Celek, and the pass got picked off by Bashaud Breeland. As Breeland started making his way back upfield, I took a few steps to the right, and the next thing I knew, I was flat on my back. I'd been blindsided by a Redskins defensive lineman. Before I even found my feet again, a massive brawl had broken out on the sidelines, resulting in both Chris Baker and our best offensive tackle, Jason Peters, being ejected from the game for unsportsmanlike conduct. The real kicker came when we saw the replay, and it showed that Breeland had never actually secured the catch. So instead of an interception, it was just an incomplete pass. I almost had my head taken off and two guys got ejected, all over a nonscoring play.

That incomplete pass, however, was a defining moment—for our team and for me. I'd taken a massive hit, but I got back up and kept fighting—not out of stubbornness or pride, but because I knew my guys were depending on me and were willing to fight for me. Look at JP. The second I went down, he had my back. We got hit hard that game, but when adversity struck, we didn't give up. We rallied around each other and fought back as a team. I threw for one more touchdown after that hit, and we ended up winning 37–34. It was the first time the Eagles had started a season 3–0 since 2004.

We won two of our next three and headed into the bye week at a solid 5–1. I put up some of the best numbers of my career the following week against Arizona, going thirty-six of sixty-two for 411 yards, but we still came up short, losing 24–20. Despite my early struggles (59.2 completion percentage, twelve touchdowns, and nine interceptions), we headed into week nine primed for a playoff run.

The game against Houston started off well. I hit Jeremy Maclin deep down the middle with a fifty-nine-yard pass for a touchdown on our second series of the game. Then, five minutes later, I tried to repeat the same play, this time targeting Riley Cooper, but I underthrew it a little, and A. J. Bouye made me pay for it with a fifty-one-yard pick six. Adding injury to insult, on our next series, with time running out in the first, Whitney Mercilus sacked me from behind. When I hit the ground, my left arm got trapped under my body, and I felt a painful cracking sensation. The trainers took me back to the locker room, where X-rays confirmed what I suspected: I'd fractured my collarbone. Mark Sanchez finished the game for us, and we won 31–21.

We were now 6–2, but my season was officially over. Initially, I thought I might be able to return by week fifteen or sixteen, but my collarbone ended up taking twelve weeks to heal, and we finished the season 10–6, missing the playoffs by one game.

When my season ended, I had thrown for 2,163 yards and had a touchdown-interception ratio of 13–10, which was quite a drop-off from the previous season's record-setting 27–2.

Looking back, I think I tried to do too much in 2014. I was trying so hard to live up to my prior accomplishments that I was putting way too much pressure on myself, and my play suffered as a result. Instead of just going with what the defense was giving me, I kept trying to force big plays—passing into heavy coverage, looking for the long ball instead of being satisfied with short-yardage passes, holding on to the ball too long in the pocket. Big plays come naturally, not by force of will. You need to stay loose. And too often that season, I was playing tight.

As a Christian, I'm a firm believer that everything in life happens for a reason, especially adversity. I think we learn more about ourselves—and about God—when we are at our weakest. I had no idea why God allowed me to suffer a broken collarbone midway through my first full season as a starter, but I knew he wanted me to learn something. I couldn't quite put words to it, but I sometimes felt like he was stretching me and allowing me to grow for something that was ahead.

Going into the off-season, I worked hard to get into the best shape of my life, and I mentally prepared myself to come back stronger than ever for the Eagles in 2015.

Then, at the gym one morning, I got that fateful phone call from Chip Kelly.

THE FINAL BLOW

NFL players often hear rumors when they're about to be traded. Sometimes the rumors are true; sometimes they aren't. In this instance, I had no idea the Eagles had been shopping me. Just like the Baker hit, I was completely blindsided.

After Chip's call, I went into a surreal fog. I honestly couldn't believe that I'd be headed anywhere but Philly.

When I saw that the call had lasted only a minute, I was really shaken. I'm a pretty relational guy, and the fact that I'd been cut loose so quickly and without warning was difficult to absorb.

You give everything you have to your team, you struggle through adversity, you work hard to come back from trials on and off the field, and then, in less time than it takes to order a pizza, your coach tells you that you've been traded.

Even though I wasn't playing the best football of my life leading up to my injury, I was 14–4 as a starter. I'd led my team to the playoffs, won MVP honors in the Pro Bowl, thrown for more than 6,700 yards and forty-six touchdowns, and set an NFL record with my touchdown-interception ratio, all of which made the whole thing even harder to understand.

I don't blame Chip. He's a good guy and a talented coach. He taught me a lot, and I loved playing for him. I just wish the situation could have been handled differently.

I knew God was trying to teach me something, but I couldn't figure out what it was. After the success of the Oakland game, I couldn't imagine not playing anymore. But once again I found myself questioning my identity as a football player. So much of who I was, how I felt, and how others perceived me was tied to the game. If I played well, I felt validated as a person. But if I played poorly, I felt inferior and incomplete.

After the initial shock of Chip's call wore off, I spent a lot of time praying, asking God to help me make sense of everything that was happening and to help me understand his plan for me. There was just so much I didn't know.

As usual, however, the NFL schedule didn't allow me much time for reflection. Tori and I had a big move coming up, and for the third time in as many years, I had a new offense to learn. I had gone to the gym that morning an Eagle, but I was leaving a Ram.

CHAPTER 5

ST. LOUIS BLUES

Different doesn't equal bad.
Different doesn't equal bad.
Different doesn't equal bad.

That's what I kept telling myself as the initial sting of the trade began to dissipate and Tori and I prepared to move to St. Louis.

Life is too short to let one surprise—even a major one—throw you completely off course. So as I entered the Gateway City, I adopted the mind-set that this was simply my next big opportunity and I was going to embrace it wholeheartedly. After all, I had the chance to play professional football, and I was one of only thirty-two guys on the planet who could say they were starting quarterbacks in the NFL. I didn't take that privilege lightly, and I had every intention of making the most of it. My collarbone was fully healed now, and thanks to a rigorous off-season training regimen, I was in the best shape of my life.

Still, there were some hurdles to overcome. Transitions in the NFL are notoriously tough. You have to show an entire organization who you are and what you can do, and you have to do it quickly.

Back in Philadelphia, everyone knew my personality. They knew my heart. They knew how much I cared about them and the game. Now I was starting from scratch. No one in St. Louis knew me. They'd seen my game film, but they hadn't seen what happened behind the scenes. They didn't know my work ethic, and they definitely didn't know my heart. I had to establish trust with my new teammates and my coaches, and that takes time.

With the start of the season less than four months away, I had a lot of work to do.

ENVIRONMENTAL CHANGE

From the moment I arrived in St. Louis, everyone was very friendly. My initial meeting with Jeff Fisher went great—he seemed like a really nice guy, and he definitely knew his football. My meetings with the rest of the coaching staff went well too. Yet I could tell instantly that I was in a different environment.

For one thing, this would be the team's last season in St. Louis. The next spring the franchise would be moving to LA, so compared to Philly, fan engagement was extremely low.

Also, the Rams were coming off a 2014 season in which the offense had been ranked twenty-first overall in points scored and twenty-eighth in total yardage in the league. I was coming from an offense that had finished the prior season ranked third and fifth in those respective categories.

What struck me most, though, was the culture within the organization. It had been more than ten years since the Rams had finished over .500, and a decade of losing seasons had taken a toll on the locker room. Simply put, the Rams weren't used to winning, and the team culture reflected that. They had a talented group of young players, but for some reason the team hadn't grown together to create a winning atmosphere.

I was committed to doing whatever I could to help turn things around, but it wasn't going to be easy. For one thing, the Rams offense didn't really play to my strengths. St. Louis ran more of an original West Coast offense, in that it didn't feature a lot of run-pass options. Basically, every play was either a run play or a pass play—period. Coach Reid and Coach Kelly both ran modified versions that allowed for more of a hybrid approach, and that's where my strengths lie—in being able to read a defense and execute the run-pass option, throw off play action, or do a plain old drop-back pass.

I was looking forward to the new challenges in front of me. The question was, would I be able to adapt to this type of play in an offense that was so different from the previous ones I'd played in?

SYSTEMS FAILURE

If the preseason was any indication of what lay ahead, we were going to be in for a long year. Personally, I played terribly. I only managed one touchdown pass—a forty-four-yarder to Chris Givens against Indianapolis—but threw two picks, one of which was returned for six. Not exactly the start I was hoping for. We emerged from the preseason 0–4, still struggling to find a rhythm on offense and about to take on a team of Super Bowl veterans.

In our first regular-season game, our offense started out literally going backward. We posted negative yardage on our first two plays and then got hit with a false start, forcing a punt from deep within our own end zone. Unfortunately, that punt went straight into the arms of Tyler Lockett, who ran it back fifty-seven yards for a touchdown, giving the Seahawks an early lead.

We managed to bounce back, and toward the end of the third, we were holding on to an eleven-point lead, courtesy of a blistering one-yard touchdown run I was able to pull off. Then the Seahawks did what they'd done all through the previous season, putting up eighteen unanswered points, including an eight-yard strip sack for a touchdown that I coughed up to cornerback Cary Williams late in the fourth.

Coming out of the two-minute warning, we were trailing 31–24. Then I hit a wide-open Lance Kendricks for a thirty-seven-yard touchdown pass with fifty-three seconds left on the clock. It was the only touchdown pass I would throw that day, but it was enough to force an overtime.

After Seattle won the coin toss, Pete Carroll took a chance on what ended up being a poorly executed onside kick. Our guys recognized it, and Bradley Marquez recovered the ball at the Seattle forty-nine, setting up a six-play drive that ended in a thirty-seven-yard field goal by Greg Zuerlein. Our defense did the rest, and we opened the season by beating the defending champions 34–31.

Overall, I had a pretty good game. I completed eighteen of twenty-seven passes for 297 yards and a 115.8 quarterback rating. Our offense, defense, and special teams all came up big when we needed them, and we found a way to win.

Three weeks later, we traveled to Arizona and gutted out a tough 24–22 win over Carson Palmer and the 3–0 Cardinals. I threw for three touchdowns, two to Tavon Austin and one to Stedman Bailey, finishing the game with 171 total passing yards.

The season was off to a decent start, even though I was still trying to find a rhythm with the offense.

In week five, we struggled against Green Bay and ended up losing 24–10. I only threw one touchdown, had a career-high four interceptions, and was sacked three times. My quarterback rating for that game was an abysmal 23.8. I knew that it takes a whole team to win or lose games, but even so, it was the ultimate example of trying to force things and create big plays out of thin air.

But as dismal as things were, the worst was yet to come.

TWENTY SECONDS

We'd just suffered a 37–13 defeat against the Bears in week ten, which dropped us to 4–5. It was the second straight loss of what would become a miserable five-game losing streak that effectively sank our season. I was in the film room meeting with our quarterbacks coach, Chris Weinke, and our two other quarterbacks, Case Keenum and Sean Mannion.

Suddenly the door swung open. Coach Fisher stood in the doorway.

"Nick," he said, "I appreciate all you've done. You're going to be with me for a long time, but at this point, we need to make a change." Then he looked at Case. "You have the keys to the team. Let's go."

And with that, he was gone. It was a twenty-second conversation—actually, a twenty-second monologue. Once again, I'd been blindsided. Two career-changing moments in a total of eighty seconds.

Needless to say, the quarterbacks room got a little weird after that. We were all shocked, including Chris. He was in a tough spot, and he didn't really know what to say. He felt bad for me, but he also had to switch gears and start getting Case ready to play against Baltimore in a few days.

"I'm sorry, Nick," Chris said. Then, turning his attention to a still-stunned Case, he said, "All right; let's go."

There's no time in the NFL to mope. Everyone has a job to do, and there's always another game around the corner. No matter what happens, the machine keeps grinding forward.

After the meeting, Case and I had a great conversation. He was one of my best friends on the team, and things got pretty emotional. They also got pretty honest. He told me how unfair this seemed and assured me that I wasn't the problem.

I knew he felt terrible. As strong a competitor as Case is, this wasn't how he wanted to get his first start of the season, and he told me as much.

"I know," I assured him. "Don't worry about me. I'll be fine. Right now we have to get you ready to face the Ravens."

I knew what it was like to come off the bench in the middle of a tough season, and I wanted to assure him he had my support. His job was to run the Rams offense; mine was to run the scout team and do whatever I could to help Case be the best he could be. Obviously, I wasn't happy about being benched, but the fact that Case and I were such good friends made the whole situation a little easier to swallow. I also recognized that one man's downfall is another's opportunity, and that helped me not to take the situation so personally.

Still, I couldn't shake the feeling of inadequacy that was creeping in. As if it weren't enough to lose my starting spot, earlier that day our strengths coach had chewed me out because I hadn't been playing well. Bad news seemed to be coming at me from all directions, and I didn't have control over any of it—where I played, how successfully I played, and most recently, *if* I played. Chip's call had set a tidal wave in motion that I felt powerless to stop. Getting benched without warning in front of Chris, Case, and Sean was just the latest reminder that my worth was measured not by heart, effort, or resilience but by numbers.

SPEAKING OF NUMBERS

Case suffered a concussion the following week against Baltimore, so I started the next two games against the Bengals and the Cardinals. It should have been an opportunity for me to shine, but I struggled in both showings, getting outscored 58–10. After Case was cleared to play, I returned to the bench for the remainder of the season.

The Rams finished the season 7–9, the team's twelfth straight season without a winning record. My numbers weren't much better. I completed a career-low 56.4 percent of my passes for 2,052 yards, seven touchdowns, and ten interceptions in eleven games for an overall quarterback rating of 69.0 (also a career low).

I barely recognized myself on the field that season. At Arizona, I was posting three-hundred- and four-hundred-yard performances with multiple touchdowns in virtually every game. Even in my rookie NFL season, I was regularly throwing for two hundred yards and eclipsed three hundred yards twice. In 2013 and 2014, I even surpassed the four-hundred-yard mark a few times. But in 2015, I felt helpless on the football field. I was once able to throw for more than 150 yards in a single quarter. Now I could barely top 150 yards passing in an entire game, and emotionally, it was starting to tear me apart.

Looking back, I should have spoken up about what I was and wasn't comfortable with. I should have had the guts to say, "There are a few plays we used to do in Philly that I feel really comfortable with. Could we try working a few of those into the offense?" But I didn't. I just did what I was told, no questions asked. Had I asserted myself more, it might have helped the team. It certainly would have helped me.

The bottom line is that I was benched because I didn't play well that season; I wasn't doing my job well enough to win. We couldn't get anything going offensively, and as the quarterback, I know that's on me.

As the 2015 season mercifully drew to a close, the same questions that had been swirling around in my mind that night in my car in East Lansing and before the Oakland game came roaring back with a vengeance:

What am I doing here?

Should I even be playing anymore?

If I quit playing football, who am I?

GOING, GOING . . .

By the end of the 2015 season, my love for the game was pretty much circling the drain, and frankly, that terrified me.

I'd never felt that way before.

When you're a kid, you play pick-up games in the park with your friends. You draw out plays in the dirt and serve as your own coach, quarterback, and referee. You don't overthink anything; you just have a blast.

In high school, you're on a team with all the guys you grew up with. You play for school pride and for the sheer love of the game.

When you get to college, the stakes go up a little, because in addition to being a game, football is also a major revenue stream, especially in Division I programs. There's more exposure, and with that comes more pressure. But it's nothing compared to the NFL.

The moment I arrived in the NFL, everything changed. I didn't notice it as much at first because I loved playing for Andy. He believed in structure and discipline, but he also trusted his players to go with their guts when they needed to. I knew he genuinely cared about me, both as a player and as a person.

But once I began achieving a certain level of success, football started to become less of a game and more of a business. I was becoming less of an individual and more of a commodity, a cog in a machine. For a relational guy like me, that was really difficult to come to grips with. Suddenly it was all a numbers game. Everything from endorsement deals to my future with the organization was contingent on my stats, my ability to produce results. As soon as I started to struggle a little in Philly, they were looking for an upgrade. While I was still trying to adapt to the Rams' style of offense, I got the hook. That's the nature of professional sports. But somewhere along the way, my self-worth got tangled up in the mix, and I was having a hard time dealing with it.

In the NFL, either you're a great quarterback or you're not. During my short tenure in the league, I had been both. The thing is, whether I was throwing four touchdowns a game or four interceptions, I was still the same guy. But that's not how I was treated—at least it didn't feel that way. When I was playing well, everybody loved me. When I wasn't, I got the vibe that I wasn't worthy of people's attention. I'm sure this is something every athlete faces, but I was really struggling.

I know I wouldn't have made it through that season with my sanity intact without my faith in Christ. The other thing that kept me grounded was spending time with Tori and Henry, our recently adopted Goldendoodle. We had gotten Henry midway through my final season in Philly, and he kept Tori company while I was away. The idea was that he would be a source of comfort for her when she wasn't feeling well, but truth be told, Henry probably provided just as much comfort for me. He didn't care what my quarterback rating was. Whether I won or lost, as soon as I walked in the door at night, he was just happy to see me. And of course Tori was a godsend—always supportive, always encouraging, and always letting me know how much she loved me. I honestly don't know what I would have done without the two of them that season.

One of the other stabilizing figures in my life during that tumultuous year was Mike Hansen, the Rams' chaplain. I would meet with Mike a few mornings a week to talk about everything I was struggling with. He encouraged me to look for ways to have a positive impact on my teammates even when I wasn't starting, and he reminded me that my gracious response in the midst of challenging times would be a testimony to others.

Around that time, I decided to keep a journal to help me process my thoughts—a habit that turned out to be extremely therapeutic. Sometimes I simply recorded what had happened that day, but a lot of times I wrote out my prayers. I'd ask questions about my life and my career, and I'd thank God for the blessings he'd brought into my life—Tori, Henry, my parents, Coach Reid, Coach Ed, Chaplain Mike, Chaplain Ted, Jason, Jon, and everyone else who'd had a positive impact on me. I thanked him for the improvement in Tori's health and for my own continued health in what can be a violent sport.

It was a helpful outlet for all of the emotions I'd kept bottled up all season. Best of all, it kept me connected with God on a daily basis. I needed to be reminded that I wasn't alone and that there was a purpose for everything I was going through—even if I still couldn't see it.

GONE

The thought of playing another year with the Rams under the conditions I'd just experienced made me cringe. I simply didn't enjoy the everyday job of playing football anymore, and on top of that, the

Rams were making it clear that I wasn't a part of their plans for the future. So while the rest of the organization was focusing on moving to LA, I went off the grid to focus on getting my mind, body, and spirit healthy again.

On April 14, the Rams pulled off a blockbuster trade with Tennessee involving nine picks spanning two seasons in order to secure the number one pick in the upcoming draft. Two weeks later, the Rams selected quarterback Jared Goff out of the University of California.

The pick didn't come as a surprise—the organization had spoken with my agent at the combine, and they said they could see if other teams were interested in me. In other words, my time with the Rams was coming to an end. Right before the draft, they offered to trade me and came close to working out a deal, but it fell through. They said they would try again during training camp, but in the meantime, they wanted me to attend off-season workouts, just in case.

When my agent asked me what I wanted to do, I told him, "Whatever it takes to get the Rams to release me, do it."

"Well," he replied, "how much are you actually willing to give away?" At the time, I still had a $1.5 million guarantee on my contract. That led to an exchange seldom heard in football.

"Everything," I said. "I'm willing to take that guarantee down to zero if it means I can be released."

Needless to say, my agent was shocked.

"I just want my freedom," I said. "That's all."

And that's exactly what I got.

On July 27, two days before veterans were scheduled to report for training camp, I was no longer with the Rams—or any NFL team, for that matter. The sense of relief I felt was almost palpable.

I'm sure most people assumed I was just another disgruntled

player who didn't like being benched and had seen the writing on the wall when Jared was drafted number one overall. But nothing could be further from the truth. The team drafting Jared had nothing to do with where I was personally. I had lost my love of the game long before Jared entered the picture, and my decision would have been the same even if they hadn't drafted Jared—or any other quarterback. And despite what some news outlets reported, I wasn't cut by the Rams; I essentially paid them for my release. I wanted the freedom to determine my own fate, even if it meant stepping away from the game.

To be honest, I didn't care what anyone else thought. All I knew was that for the first time since I'd entered the NFL, I was able to call the shots about my career. I was no longer contractually obligated to anyone. I finally had a choice in where I wanted to play—or *if* I wanted to play.

For the first time in four years, I felt free.

So that summer, while everyone else headed off to training camp to get ready for the 2016 season, I headed into the wilderness—to go fly-fishing.

CHAPTER 6

INTO THE WILDERNESS

Once Tori's brother Ryan heard about my newfound freedom, he didn't waste any time. An avid camper, Ryan had been trying for years to get me to go on one of his family's annual backpacking and fly-fishing trips.

"Now that you have some free time on your hands," Ryan said, "you should go backpacking with me."

I didn't take much convincing. "When can we go?"

He cocked his head and smiled. "Funny you should mention it. I have a trip with my wife's family coming up in a few weeks. Would you like to come?"

Normally, a vacation in July wouldn't even be an option. Right around this time, I'd be packing my bags and leaving for training camp. But not this year. For once, my summer schedule was wide open.

"I'm in."

I was looking forward to hanging out with Ryan, and even more than that, I was eager to catch my breath. I'd been on the NFL treadmill for four years, and I figured going off the grid for a few days would be a welcome change. As it turned out, God had a plan for that week that went well beyond me getting some R & R.

GOING OFF THE GRID

Before I headed out, I had a few phone calls to make. First, I needed to talk to my dad and my father-in-law, Dan, and tell them I was done playing football. Those were going to be tough conversations because I knew how much joy it brought them to watch me play. But they also knew how difficult the past season had been for me.

I was especially dreading telling my dad. He had loved watching me play sports since I was a little kid, and I knew how much he would miss that.

My dad has always been one of my heroes. The guy is a perfect example of what you can accomplish with grit and determination. He didn't have many educational opportunities, but he worked harder than anyone I know to make it in the restaurant business. As a kid, I remember him coming home at midnight smelling like a kitchen, but he never complained. Neither did my mother. I never realized how much my parents had given up for my sisters and me until I got older. That made it all the more difficult to break the news that my career was suddenly over. But I didn't try to sugarcoat it—I just told him the truth.

"Dad," I said, "I can't play anymore. My greatest strength has always been playing with all my heart, and now that's gone. My love for the game has vanished, and I can't go on like that."

He seemed to understand, but I had a suspicion he was hoping I'd change my mind.

As it turned out, he wasn't the only one.

As soon as the Rams released me, a bunch of teams—including the Kansas City Chiefs, where Andy Reid was now coaching—contacted my agent. After my release went public, Andy and I chatted several times about the possibility of my playing in KC. I'd been transparent with him about my struggles, both professional and personal, and he understood where I was coming from. I had no intention of playing next season, but I promised him I'd think about it over the next few days. He said that if I changed my mind, there'd be a spot for me with the Chiefs.

A few nights before the trip, Ryan and I went to a local REI store so I could load up on a few essentials. For Ryan, this was like Christmas in July. He had a blast helping me get everything I needed. In fact, had he been an REI salesperson, he would have made a pretty sweet commission that night.

I hadn't been camping since I was a kid, so I went all out—backpack, tent, sleeping bag, sleeping pad. Ryan took particular pleasure in teasing me about my new deluxe backpack, complete with a built-in solar panel to charge my phone via a USB cord. It wasn't exactly regulation Cub Scout equipment, but who doesn't need a phone charger while roughing it in the great outdoors?

Besides, this was an investment. Now that I was finished with football, I figured there would be a lot of camping trips with Ryan in my future.

The day of our departure, I said my good-byes to Tori, and then Ryan and I left from his house in Costa Mesa at five o'clock in the morning. It was a five-hour drive to our destination—a trailhead called the Forks of the Kern, located on the Upper Kern River in the southern Sierra Nevada Mountains. This was officially off the grid.

For the first two hours of the drive, the major topic of discussion was my career.

"If Andy Reid believes in you, why don't you give it another shot?" Ryan asked. "It seems like an ideal environment for you to rekindle your love of the game. If you still aren't enjoying it, even under Andy, then you can step away for good. But at least you'll have tried. What do you have to lose?"

I appreciated what Ryan was trying to do. Like the rest of my family, he was convinced I'd made my decision prematurely, and he didn't want me to have any regrets. But as much as I hated feeling like I was letting them all down, my decision was made. It was time for me to step away from football. It was time for the next chapter of my life to begin, and I was okay with that.

About three hours into the trip, Ryan and I stopped at a McDonald's in a tiny desert town called Mojave. After stretching my legs a bit and stopping in the restroom, I went back to the car while Ryan ordered some breakfast. I knew we were about to lose cell phone reception for the weekend, so I sent a long text to Coach Reid with my final decision: I was officially hanging up my cleats. I thanked him for drafting me, for giving me the opportunity to live out my dream, for being a father figure to me, and for believing in me. I wanted him to know how grateful I was.

Then I shot Tori a quick text to let her know what I'd done.

When Ryan got back to the car, I told him about the text I'd sent to Coach Reid. He was incredulous. He even jokingly threatened to suspend my phone privileges. After we drove out a few more miles, the diminished reception made Ryan's threat a reality, so I powered down my phone and packed it away for the weekend. I wouldn't be needing that solar-panel charger after all.

As far as I was concerned, I had officially retired from the NFL.

BACK TO BASICS

As we rolled along, the landscape slowly morphed from desert brown to forest green. In the tiny town of Kernville, about ninety minutes from our destination, we stopped at the local fly shop to pick up the additional fly-fishing gear I needed. The woman at the desk didn't recognize me, and that was a relief. I was happy to be just any guy going fishing for the week.

When we arrived at the trailhead, it was about eleven in the morning, and even at an altitude of six thousand feet, it was hot. About an hour into our two-and-a-half-mile hike down a fairly steep descent into a canyon, I realized that I'd forgotten to bring the fishing gear from the fly shop. Total rookie move.

Ryan just looked at me. "Well, there's no way we're trekking all the way back to the car. You can just use some of my stuff."

I was kicking myself, but I figured there would be plenty of opportunities to use my gear in the future. After all, this was just the first of hundreds of trips like this.

Eventually we met up with the rest of our group, which included eight other people, all relatives of Ryan's wife, Krystal. Ryan's father-in-law, Bob, and his uncle Mike had taken backpacking trips to that part of the Kern River for more than forty years, and they had passed on their passion to the rest of the family.

It was easy to see why they loved it so much. The Forks of the Kern is breathtakingly beautiful. Being deep in the woods—miles away from cell phone service, skyscrapers, and all the technology of our modern existence—helped me to relax and appreciate God's majesty. It didn't hurt that there were no complicated new offenses to master, no grueling rehab sessions, no trade negotiations. Being out in the big, beautiful world God made reminded me that there's more to life than football.

Every day was picture perfect, although no camera could do justice to the scenery. Crisp mornings gave way to sunny, cloudless afternoons—although I wouldn't have minded a few clouds, because it was crazy hot out there. The daytime temperature hovered around the one-hundred-degree mark the entire weekend. But at least it was a dry heat. (In West Coast vernacular, that means, "You'll still be baked like a Thanksgiving turkey, just without the additional basting of East Coast humidity.")

The Kern River itself is a fairly wide freestone river. The scattered boulders and gentle turns throughout the canyon create some great fly-fishing runs for Kern River rainbow trout, a species native to that river.

Ryan said I caught on quickly to fly-fishing, and while I'm inclined to take his word for it, I wouldn't bother watching out for me on any of those fishing tournaments on TV. Over the course of the entire weekend, I caught a whopping two trout to Ryan's dozen. Still, I had a blast.

Dinners consisted of steaks and veggies cooked on a portable stove, and breakfast was usually bacon and eggs, and of course, Bulletproof coffee. Being a self-confessed coffee snob, I need my Bulletproof coffee . . . the way a rainbow trout needs water. I might have forgotten my fishing tackle, but there's no way I could have forgotten my coffee. By the end of the trip, I believe I even converted a few souls to my morning brew of choice.

The nights were beautiful and almost eerily quiet. For the past several years, I'd had coaches critiquing me, teammates looking up to me, sixty thousand fans cheering all around me, reporters asking me tough questions, and radio hosts contacting me with endless requests. And now I was experiencing virtual silence. The biggest commotion we encountered during the day was a rustling leaf or two, and in the evening we were lulled to sleep by the soft rippling of the Kern.

Each night I opened the canopy of my tent to gaze at the stars and to talk to God. It was incredibly therapeutic. Out in the wilderness, I was no longer a football player; I was just Nick. I didn't have to study a playbook. I didn't have to train. I didn't have to get ready for the next season. I could simply enjoy myself in the woods with family and friends. I loved every minute of it—even with the blistering heat and my lowly pair of trout.

On the way home, Ryan and I didn't say much about football. We mostly talked about the trip—most notably, my championship-caliber fly-fishing skills. When we got near Kernville, our cell service returned, and when I powered my phone back up, I had a boatload of text messages waiting for me. One was from Coach Reid, and as usual, he was very gracious. He reiterated that he understood my decision but wanted to make sure I knew there would always be a place for me on his team if I wanted it.

I read his message to Ryan. At the time, I didn't think anything of my reaction to Coach Reid's words. But Ryan told me later that when I read the text aloud, he noticed something different in my tone. It was the first time he thought I might actually play again.

A MOMENT OF CLARITY

I arrived home to find reality waiting in the doorway, impatiently tapping its foot. I suppose it was to be expected—you can't just drop out of the NFL cold turkey and assume there won't be any residual effects. Six teams had called my agent while I was away, expressing interest in signing me. Then my family launched their second assault.

"You can't just step away from the game without giving it one more shot," they kept saying.

When I returned home from the trip, Tori gave me a heartfelt, four-page typed letter. In it, she talked about our relationship, everything we'd gone through together, and how much she loved me. Then she encouraged me to try playing one more time. She said that if I still felt the same way after one season, I should feel free to walk away. But she didn't want me to spend the rest of my life wondering, *What if . . . ?*

What's happening? I asked myself. One moment I was free as a bird in the Sierra Nevadas, and the next I felt like a bear caught in a trap. I had told everyone clearly that I didn't want to play anymore, but somehow they weren't getting the message. Wasn't I allowed to stop playing? This was *my* life. Why didn't I get a say?

I knew my family was trying to be supportive, and they wanted to make sure I wasn't making an emotional decision I would regret later. Yet I couldn't help feeling like they were trying to push their own agenda for my future. I just wanted the pressure to stop.

Two nights after I got back from my trip, Tori and I were sitting on the patio of my parents' vacation home in Southern California. It was a beautiful evening, and I should have been rested and refreshed after my time in the Sierra Nevadas, but at that moment I was not a happy camper.

Tori and I weren't on the same page about my future, and it was time for a candid conversation.

"You know I'll support you whatever you decide," she said. "But I feel like you're hanging it up for the wrong reasons."

That wasn't what I wanted to hear. I felt like she was forcing my hand, trying to talk me out of a decision I'd already made.

"I don't want you to stop doing something you used to love because of one bad year," she went on. "I'd hate for you to look back with regret and have a sour taste in your mouth about football forever. What if there's more that God has planned for you in this role?"

After some tears from both of us, there wasn't much else to say. Where do you go when you've hit a relational roadblock? It was clear that more talking wasn't going to convince either of us to change our minds, so we did the only thing we could think of: we prayed.

God, I don't know what to do, I prayed silently. *From a human perspective, I don't want to play football anymore. But I also know this is about more than what I want. I need to trust you with all I have.*

If there was anyone who could help me fall in love with the game again, I knew it was Coach Reid. But I didn't know if I had the strength to go back.

I keep telling everyone this is my decision, but it's not, I went on. *This is about following the path you've laid out before me. It's about doing what you want me to do. Please, God, help me to see your plan more clearly. Help me to make a decision that will glorify you.*

At that moment, as I sat there praying next to my wife, I felt a sudden sense of clarity. I knew that if I was going to play again, it would take complete faith and trust in God. The only way this would work was if he gave me the strength, the ability, and the joy I would need. Deciding to play again would be the tougher road, but it would also result in the most growth.

I wasn't sure whether I had what it took, but I believed God could get me there.

IDENTITY CRISIS

For years, my identity had been inextricably tied to football, and when I got to the NFL, that only escalated. I know I'm not the only one who has experienced this—we're all tempted to measure our worth by what we do, whether it's athletics or a job of any kind. But when we view ourselves solely in light of our accomplishments, we create a false reality, because we are more than what can be written on a stat sheet. There's so much more to a person than how far they can throw or how hard they can hit.

When you measure your worth based on what other people say about you or on what you can achieve, it's hard to understand who you really are. It took the nightmare of the 2015 season to remind me that my identity is in Christ, not in what I can do on a football field.

Ultimately I had to separate Nick Foles the person from Nick Foles the football player, and it took stepping away from football— even if only for a short time—to make that separation happen.

Now there were two clearly defined paths stretching out in front of me: to play football or not. I felt stuck. Everything in me was telling me to hang it up, but the people around me kept urging me to give it another shot. For weeks all those voices were echoing in my head so loudly that I couldn't hear the most important voice of all— and the only one that really mattered. It wasn't until that night, when Tori and I stopped talking and began to pray, that I experienced a moment of calm. That's when everything finally became clear.

When my identity was tied to football, I constantly felt the pressure to be perfect. I lost sight of the fact that I don't have to be perfect—in fact, I *can't* be perfect. No one can. Only Jesus is perfect. I also don't have to throw twenty-seven touchdowns and only two interceptions every season to be successful. The true measure of success is to make sure everything I do—the way I act, the way I treat others, the way I deal with disappointment and setbacks— reflects and glorifies God. God doesn't care whether I throw forty touchdowns in a season or none. His love isn't contingent on my performance on the field. It's unconditional.

As a Christian, I find my identity, value, and purpose in life in one source—God. He's the one who created me. He's the one who gifted me with my athletic abilities. He's the one who led me from Michigan State to Arizona, and in doing so, led me to Tori. Everything I have comes from him. And everything I am is because of him.

I'm not just a football player. I'm a child of God who happens to be called to play football, using the gifts and abilities he has blessed me with. And that's a huge distinction.

Once I finally understood this, I realized that it didn't really matter which path I chose. There wasn't a right or wrong decision. Whether or not I continued to play football wouldn't change the way God felt about me. He would love me no matter what I did, and the main thing he wanted from me was that I love him and trust him with all my heart.

It's ironic, really. That whole time I was trying so hard to please everyone else, when all I really needed to do was to please God. And I could do that anywhere, in any profession.

The paralysis was finally over. I had a phone call to make.

GETTING BACK IN THE GAME

As soon as I realized which step I wanted to take, I got up from the patio and walked out to the street, where nobody could hear me. Then I called Andy Reid.

"Coach," I said, "I want to give it one more shot. I can still do this, and I'm willing to give it everything I have. I don't care that the other teams are offering me more money—you're the only coach I want to play for right now."

Andy didn't miss a beat. "I'm all for it, Nick. Let's get this thing rolling."

The two of us might have agreed, but things aren't that simple in the NFL. As an unsigned player, you can't just show up at training camp and say, "Hey, get me a helmet. I want to play." Phone calls have to be made, numbers have to be crunched, and papers have to be signed—*a lot* of papers. So as soon as I hung up with Andy, I called my agent, informed him of my decision (which he was thrilled to hear about), and asked him to get the contract process started.

When I walked back to the house, Tori was on the patio. She thought I'd gone to make an official retirement call.

This was going to be sweet.

"So," I said as casually as possible, "what do you think Evan and Ryan are doing right now?"

She looked at me, her face blank. "Huh?"

"What do you think your brothers are doing?"

She had no idea where I was going with this.

She just shook her head. "I have no idea. Why?"

"Well," I said, trying to fight back a smile, "I need them to catch for me."

Tori froze. The look on her face was priceless. "What?"

"Well, if I'm going to do this training camp thing, I need to be able to throw."

"Are you serious?"

"Yep." I leaned toward her and smiled. "We're heading to Kansas City. I'm going to give this one more shot."

Tori threw her arms around me. We called our parents, and they were thrilled. Then we called Evan and Ryan. Once they finished whooping, they said they'd be more than willing to be my throwing buddies that night.

By the time we found a youth sports field in Newport Beach that was still lit, it was almost nine o'clock. But I didn't have any time to lose. NFL training camps had already started, and I hadn't thrown a football in months. For almost an hour, Evan and Ryan ran every route I asked them to run, including slants, hitches, comebacks, daggers, posts, and, of course, the go ball. I was a little rusty at first, and my timing was definitely off on a few throws, but I was glad to discover that my arm still worked.

As I tossed a combination of perfect and not-so-perfect spirals to my brothers-in-law under a moonlit sky, I couldn't help but reflect on everything that had transpired and everything that was about to take place. God was leading me into a new chapter in my life, which was both exciting and scary.

But do you know how you defeat fear? You don't punt, call an audible, or try to run an end-around. You face it head-on. You run straight at it—not with your own power, but with a power far greater than yourself. Fear doesn't come from God. And when God is with you, there is nothing *to* fear.

Even so, as Ryan ran one final deep post route and I watched the ball sail about a foot and a half over his head, there was a part of me that couldn't help but wonder, *What have I just gotten myself into?*

CHAPTER 7

CHIEF CONCERN

In *A League of Their Own*, a movie about the World War II–era All-American Girls Professional Baseball League, Tom Hanks utters one of the most iconic sports-movie lines of all time.

His character, Jimmy Dugan—manager for the Rockford Peaches—chews out one of his players for a defensive lapse, and she starts sobbing. Indignantly, he reprimands her from the dugout, "There's no crying in baseball!"

Most people think there's no crying in football either. Well, think again.

On the fourth day of training camp with the Kansas City Chiefs, I broke down in tears. It was a little after six o'clock in the morning, and I was writing in my journal when I just lost it. I put down my pen, leaned back in my chair in one of the dorm rooms at Missouri Western State University, and had a good cry.

But they weren't tears of sadness. I was crying out of excitement and gratitude—and maybe even a little awe.

There was nothing particularly special about my fourth day in training camp. I think that's just how long it took for me to absorb everything that had happened over the past couple of weeks.

As I reflected in my dorm-room chair, I took a quick self-inventory and was amazed to discover how much my perspective had changed since leaving St. Louis.

Yes, I wanted to study film.

Yes, I wanted to do footwork and throwing drills.

Yes, I wanted to study the playbook.

Yes, I wanted to be in the huddle.

I actually wanted to play football again!

Notice that my shocking realization arrived on the *fourth* day of camp. The first few days were characterized more by feelings that ranged anywhere from "somewhat concerned" to "DEFCON 1."

I was excited about the prospect of playing for Andy (or Big Red, as most of his players call him), but I knew there were no guarantees. I still had to earn my spot on the roster like everyone else, and trying to learn a new playbook and establish a rhythm with a new set of tight ends, wide receivers, and running backs after barely even touching a football all spring was going to be a tall order.

Fortunately, I had a great offensive coordinator in Matt Nagy. I knew Matt from my rookie year with the Eagles, where he was a quality-control assistant to Doug Pederson. He welcomed me in from the first day, even letting me use his vehicle during training camp. I could hardly believe it—I hadn't even secured a spot on the roster yet, and here I was driving around town in the OC's vehicle. Is it any wonder I wanted to play for these guys?

Don't get me wrong: going hard for up to thirteen hours a day, six days a week, for six straight weeks is no stroll in the park. And since I arrived at camp late and somewhat unexpectedly, they didn't have the proper equipment on hand for me. As a result, my first few days were spent wearing wide receiver shoulder pads (which sit more heavily on your shoulders, making them pretty uncomfortable to throw in) and different cleats than I was used to. In spite of all this, I was having a blast. In part, I can thank my brother-in-law Evan for that.

Evan Moore played five seasons in the NFL (2008–2012) with Cleveland, Seattle, and Philadelphia. When I started to hit the wall during training camp, I gave Evan a call so I could unload some of what I was going through. I usually reach out to him for advice when I have a football situation I'm dealing with. What he told me that night changed everything for me.

"Nick," he told me, "everyone wants to quit football at training camp." He was joking—mostly—but it made me feel better to know I wasn't the only one struggling.

It seemed like all the other players thought training camp was the greatest experience of their lives. Meanwhile, I was thinking, *Man, this is so hard.* The grind of training camp was seriously testing my resolve. And I felt so guilty about it—like I didn't fully appreciate the opportunity I'd been given to play in the NFL, or worse, that I didn't deserve to be there. But as soon as Evan assured me that everyone else felt the same way, it was like getting a huge lineman off my back.

Being open and honest—especially when it comes to areas of weakness—has always been really important to me, for that exact reason. Too often people put up a front, acting like everything is fine, even when it isn't. They hide what's bothering them because they don't want anyone to know they don't have it all together—that they're not perfect.

Professional athletes are especially guilty of this. No matter how badly they might be hurt or what's going on behind the scenes in their personal lives, their natural tendency is to act tough and put up a Superman-like facade. It's kind of funny, really—we don't hesitate to go head-to-head with a three-hundred-pound defender, but we're terrified of being perceived as weak. And to most athletes, especially those in the NFL, weakness is perhaps the worst liability.

Personally, I couldn't disagree more. Being transparent about what you're thinking and feeling and struggling with is actually the healthier way to live. When we share our faults and weaknesses, not only are we being honest, we also become more relatable—and more human—to the people around us.

It's possible to be part of a team or a family or a group of friends and still be isolated. We hide our faults and weaknesses, and in doing so, we only end up feeling alone. On top of that, we create a false reality that makes everyone else who is struggling feel isolated as well.

Vulnerability is hard for all of us to live out, and when it comes to football, it's not exactly something you're trained to do in practice. But when Evan admitted how hard training camp was, I didn't think less of him. On the contrary, I thought more highly of him. It takes real courage and strength of character to admit your weaknesses. His confession relieved me of the guilt I'd been carrying around, which in turn made me a more relaxed and productive player.

I'd love to take credit for the revelation that we can find strength in the midst of our weakness, but the truth is, that idea actually dates way back to before the invention of football.

Scripture says there's great strength in human weakness. Our frailty and inabilities highlight God's perfect strength. Jesus himself is the ultimate example of finding strength in weakness. He was fully God and fully human, yet he came down to serve others and sacrifice himself for us. What appeared to be a moment of weakness for him was actually the strongest moment in history. He gave his life for us—not because he had to, but because he chose to, because he loves us.

When we are at our most vulnerable, that's when we tend to pray and ask God for help. Why don't we pray like that when things are going well? It's because we think we can do it on our own and through our own strength. In reality, however, we are strongest when we are weak, because that's when we turn to God and put our trust in him. It seems counterintuitive, but I knew that my greatest strength would come not when I thought I had it all together but when I knew how much I needed God—whether things were going well or not.

Grasping these foundational biblical concepts and applying them revolutionized my life—and my career.

BIG RED

The other thing that made training camp more bearable for me that year was being reunited with Coach Reid. In an often callous, chaotic profession, he was one of the few kind and consistent presences in my life. He was the first person in the NFL who believed in me, and that belief has never wavered—even when I was coming off the worst season of my career.

After a tumultuous year in St. Louis, it felt great to be back in Coach Reid's system again. His offense was a good fit for me, and I was surprised how many of the old plays I remembered. Plus, like most athletes, I crave familiarity and discipline, and Coach Reid provided plenty of opportunities for both. His schedule was demanding, but he also honored our time with our families. We knew exactly what was expected of us, both as athletes and as individuals. And because Andy invested so much time and love in me, I wanted to do the same for him.

I had no idea how much playing time I'd see that year, but one thing I did know was that no matter what happened, I would give Coach Reid my very best.

C-H-I-E-F-S

Going into training camp, I knew my role: I was the backup for Alex Smith. Alex was a thirty-two-year-old veteran coming off another strong season, having led the Chiefs to their second playoff season since he arrived in Kansas City via a trade in 2013. I had met him at the Pro Bowl and we really hit it off, so I was looking forward to playing together.

Earlier in my career, I told Tori I didn't think I'd ever be able to be a backup. At the time, I didn't consider that arrogant. Like most athletes, I just wanted to be out on the field rather than standing on the sidelines. Heading into this season, though, I had a totally different mind-set. I didn't have to be in the number one spot to feel validated. Andy knew who I was as a person, and he knew what I was capable of as a player—and so did I. That was enough.

Ironically, by the time I arrived at training camp, the only jersey number left was number 1. I never liked wearing that number, and that season it seemed like even more of a mismatch. As it happened, one of the younger wide receivers had pulled number 4, which was Tori's number when she played volleyball at Arizona. When I told him about everything Tori and I had gone through, he agreed to a trade. I was no longer number 1, and that was fine by me. My job that year was simple: to work hard, support Alex as best I could, encourage my teammates, be a positive influence in the locker room, and be ready to step in and play if needed. On a deeper level, my goal was to glorify God in everything I did, and to do it with a joyful spirit.

This was surprisingly easy to do, in large part because being around Alex and the other guys was so much fun. I enjoyed observing Alex's work ethic, his meticulous planning, and his style of play. We prepared for every game together, and spending all that time with him allowed me to get firsthand mentoring from a veteran quarterback.

A typical week with Alex included physical workouts, fundamental drill work, meetings, and film review—all the typical stuff—but Alex had a very regimented schedule. He would study the film, determine exactly what he needed to do to prepare for that week's defense, and zero in on that. He was focused and task oriented, and not a single moment of preparation was wasted.

Alex had a family, and he wasn't going to hang around the practice facility or the weight room until ten o'clock at night. His goal was to do everything he needed to do to prepare in a timely manner, then go home to his wife and kids. Most of the guys I'd been around before had a "first one in, last one out" mentality. There's nothing wrong with that—Alex just worked exceptionally hard to maintain a healthy work-life balance. He taught me a lot that year, but one of the best lessons was how to excel on the field while still making family your top priority.

It wasn't all hard work, though. Alex, Tyler Bray, Joel Stave, and I also had a lot of fun together that season. There was a basketball hoop in the locker room, and any chance we got—before meetings, between meetings, after meetings—we'd be out there shooting. It was the first time in my career that I was able to bring my two favorite sports together under one roof, and I loved it.

We also had a cool tradition on Thursday nights. Once meetings and film prep were done at around six o'clock, we'd head back to the locker room and play a game of H-O-R-S-E, except we renamed it C-H-I-E-F-S, and you couldn't just shoot. Every shot had to be a trick shot. You had to ricochet it off the wall, bank it in, balance on one leg, shoot behind your back—the weirder the better. It was a blast.

After that, we'd run home, take a quick shower, and go out with our wives for a special quarterbacks dinner. Every week we'd pick a different restaurant, eat dinner, hang out for a couple of hours, and enjoy talking with each other. It was a way for us to bond as teammates and to build friendships outside the facility with other couples in a similar life stage. That year Tori and I even celebrated Thanksgiving with Alex, his wife, Liz, and their kids, along with Tyler and Jen Bray and Joel Stave.

Honestly, everything about that season reminded me of family— and the best news was yet to come.

A MAJOR SURPRISE

"Hey, when are you going to be home?"

Tori sounded anxious—kind of strange, actually.

That's weird, I thought. *She knows I'll be home as soon as we're done.*

In her defense, on that particular day, our film session was running a bit longer than usual. We were playing the 7–3 Broncos that Sunday, so we'd been devoting some extra time to breaking down their defense.

"I'm almost done," I told her.

"Well, come home quickly. I'm getting hungry."

"All right. I'll be there soon."

Fifteen minutes later, as I was driving home, she called again. "Are you almost here?"

This wasn't like her at all. I was starting to get a little freaked out. "I'm almost home. Are you okay?"

She assured me she was fine, but frankly I didn't know what was going on.

When I got home, Tori was in the kitchen making dinner and Henry was lying on the couch. She seemed fine, so after I said hello, I went to get a quick snack. It had been a long day, and I was exhausted.

That's when Tori said, "Give Henry a hug."

"In a minute," I told her. "I just want to grab a snack to hold me over until dinner."

"No," she insisted, "go and give Henry a hug."

Now things were really getting bizarre. *What in the world is going on?*

"Okay," I said, trying to hide my annoyance.

When I bent over to give Henry a hug, I noticed something under his paw. It was long, slender, and white, and seemed to be made out of plastic. My first reaction was, *Why is my dog holding a tampon?* On closer inspection, however, I saw that it was a pregnancy test. My mind went blank.

We hadn't even been talking about having a baby. Given Tori's health problems, we were planning to wait until the off-season to talk to her doctor about the feasibility of her even getting pregnant. So until that moment, having a baby was the last thing on my mind.

"We're pregnant?" I asked, a smile spreading across my face.

"Yes!" Her eyes welled up with tears.

I was completely overwhelmed—both of us were. All we could do was hold each other and cry while poor Henry just stared at us, wagging his tail and wondering what all the fuss was about.

We already had five nieces in the family, so we felt a certain amount of pressure to have a boy. "We can't wait until the due date," I told Tori. "We have to find out if we're having a boy or a girl."

She agreed, so as soon as she hit the ten-week mark, we got the blood test. But we didn't look at the results right away—we wanted to do something special to find out the gender.

We decided to go to a doughnut shop and give them our test results. They would give us a dozen doughnuts—glazed pink or blue, depending on the gender.

We waited until we got back to the house to open the box. It was only a fifteen-minute drive, but it felt like an eternity.

When we opened the box, the donuts were all pink.

I stared at Tori in disbelief. Another girl in the family! We were both thrilled. There was more hugging, then more crying. Poor Henry.

After we got ahold of ourselves again, Tori had a confession to make. "I knew it was a girl."

"What do you mean?" I asked.

"When they gave us the box, I saw pink frosting on the side. I wiped it off so you wouldn't see it."

I laughed. *That's my girl.*

Once we knew we were having a girl, it was time to think about a name. My dad originally wanted to name me Willy, and I started testing out names that rhymed. When I landed on Lily, Tori and I both loved it. Tori's dad's middle name is James, and we liked the sound of the two names together. That cinched it—our daughter's name would be Lily James.

Tori and I got such a kick out of the pink doughnuts that when it came time to reveal Lily's gender to the rest of the family, we wanted to do something special for them, too. At this point it was early December, and Kansas City was covered in a blanket of snow. We went out to a gated field near Alex Smith's house where we would go sometimes to throw the tennis ball to Henry. We put two cardboard boxes in the middle of the field—one marked "boy" and the other marked "girl"—along with matching pink and blue balloons. Then we put dog treats behind the "girl" box, and with the camera rolling, instructed Henry to tell our family members whether the baby was a boy or a girl.

Like a good boy, Henry took off like a shot, and after wandering back and forth between the boxes for a few minutes, he eventually found his treats behind the girl box.

Way to build the suspense, buddy.

That little guy was going to be a great big brother.

BENCH RESTORATION

The 2016 season with the Chiefs was a lot of fun for me, even if most of it was from the sidelines.

I saw my first action in week eight after Alex took a nasty hit to the head in the opening drive against Indianapolis. It was the first time I'd taken the field since I stepped in for Case Keenum in week twelve of the previous season, when he got hurt in the game against the Ravens. Considering it had been almost a year since I'd seen game-time action, I did pretty well, hitting Tyreek Hill deep down the middle for forty-nine yards before connecting with Travis Kelce in the end zone for fourteen yards early in the second quarter. Alex came back in for the following series, and after several stalled drives, he hit one of my old teammates from Philly, Jeremy Maclin, in the end zone to put us up 14–7 at the half.

Alex started the third quarter but ended up leaving the game again—this time for good—after taking another hit to the head in the opening drive of the second half. I finished out the game, completing sixteen of twenty-two passes overall for 223 total yards, including a thirty-four-yard touchdown pass to Tyreek late in the third.

We ended up winning that game 30–14. The fact that Alex and I were able to tag-team so effectively was a testament to the synergy we'd created in the opening months of the season. Like I said, football is football; you can play anywhere. The guys you play with make all the difference.

With Alex still out, I started the following week against Jacksonville. While my numbers weren't quite as impressive—twenty of thirty-three for 187 yards and one touchdown—we won that game 19–14, putting us at 6–2 midway through the season.

Alex finished the rest of the season, leading us to a 12–4 record and an AFC West title. We ended up losing to the Steelers in a nail-biter game in the divisional round (18–16), but overall we had a really strong season. Even though I played less in this season than in any other in my career, it was without question one of my all-time favorites. And as a highly competitive guy, I was more surprised about that than anyone.

Although I never pictured myself as a backup, I genuinely loved playing behind Alex—helping him, growing in our friendship, and watching him succeed. It was humbling and rewarding all at once.

After St. Louis, I'd needed a bounce-back year in a big way. Of course, an athlete's comeback year is usually accompanied by big statistical performances, personal awards, and maybe even a championship. My bounce-back year happened while I remained mostly on the sidelines, yet I experienced more joy than I had in any other season. The fact that God restored my love of the game under those circumstances shows just how much he had changed my heart.

Even though my playing time was limited, I was still able to have an impact in the locker room by supporting and encouraging my teammates. That season I spent a lot of time developing relationships with those guys and really investing in them. Because of what I'd accomplished in 2013, I had earned their respect, so when I shared about the struggles I'd gone through in 2015 and how I'd almost quit the game, my words carried some weight. Not surprisingly, some of my teammates were wrestling with the same issues, and it felt good to know that God was using my hard times to help other people.

Now that I was starting to become a little more vocal about my faith, I wanted to dig deeper into what I believed. I'd been participating in Bible studies since my days at Arizona with Coach Ed, and I'd even helped lead team studies in Philly. I knew enough to impact my teammates, but I also knew there was a lot more I needed to learn.

Every Friday morning that season, I met with Phillip Kelley, the team chaplain, and at one point I mentioned to him that I'd been thinking about going to seminary after I retired. I tossed around the idea of becoming a youth pastor so I could speak into kids' lives the way people like Pastor Ted, Mike Hansen, and others had spoken into mine.

When I asked him about seminary programs, he told me about his time at Liberty University and how he'd worked as founder Jerry Falwell Sr.'s personal intern for a time. I also found out that the NFL offers players $20,000 a year for tuition reimbursement. This felt like divine providence. By going to seminary, I could grow deeper in my faith, broaden my knowledge of Scripture, and set myself up for a career after football, all at the same time.

When I left Arizona, I'd promised myself that would be the end of textbooks for me. I never wanted to go back to school again. And yet, by the time the 2016 season had drawn to a close, I was signed up for two seminary classes through Liberty's online program—one in the winter semester and one in the spring. If that isn't evidence of God at work, I don't know what is.

GREENER PASTURES

After the 2016 season ended, Andy and I met for about an hour to talk about 2017. When I signed with Kansas City, it was a one-year deal worth $1.75 million that included a second-year option worth around $6.75 million, depending on my performance in 2016.

Naturally, I told Andy I wanted to come back and play for him again. Tori and I both loved living in Kansas City. We'd become very close to the Smiths and the Brays, and I'd developed a lot of good relationships with other players on the team. I genuinely enjoyed playing behind Alex, and of course, I loved playing for Andy.

Andy said he wanted me back too, but unfortunately, it wasn't up to the two of us. We would have to wait and see what management wanted to do—and like most deals in the NFL, it was going to come down to money. To be honest, even *I* thought my second-year option was a little pricey. But I was still hopeful.

By March 9, 2017—the first day of the new league year—the details of my contract had yet to be decided. I was calling my agent almost daily for updates. I even offered to renegotiate the option figure to give Kansas City a hometown discount. A few days later, my agent called to tell me that the Chiefs were not going to pick up my option. Even with the hometown discount, there wasn't enough cap space available to make it work. That said, we were trying to work out a new one-year deal that would be fair for both sides. There was some back and forth, and when they finally made me an offer, it wasn't good for both parties. There were no hard feelings, but unfortunately this is just part of the business.

After discussing it with Tori and spending some time in prayer, I decided to take a leap of faith and decline the offer, sending me into new territory as a free agent. I still wasn't giving up hope, though. Even as my agent and I expanded our search, we continued to work with Kansas City on coming up with a number that would work for both of us. I even renegotiated my original hometown discount, which was already, by NFL terms, ridiculously low. That's how much I loved playing there. But in the end, to our mutual disappointment, we just couldn't find a way to make it work.

NFL contract negotiations are a strange business. Contracts show what teams think of you, and players get labeled by the deals they sign. If you sign a good deal, teams will say, "Man, this guy is thought of highly," and it can help you down the road. Sign a team-friendly deal, and it could negatively typecast you in the future.

But as Tori and I discussed our future, we knew money wasn't the object. We were already more blessed than we ever expected to be. Our biggest priority was finding the best possible place for our soon-to-be-expanding family.

After negotiations broke down with Kansas City, there were only two other teams firmly in the running: Philadelphia and Tampa Bay. Both offers made it clear that they wanted me there to help improve the backup situation and mentor a young quarterback. In Philly, I'd be behind Carson Wentz, the second overall pick of the 2016 draft. In Tampa Bay, I'd be backing up Jameis Winston, the Buccaneers' number one overall pick from 2015.

To be honest, the offer from the Eagles came as a total surprise. If you could have eavesdropped on my inner monologue at that time, it probably would have sounded something like this:

Wow, the Eagles want me back.

Yeah, but they traded me.

It's a strong offer.

Yeah, but they traded me.

The coaching staff involved in that trade is no longer there.

Yeah, but they traded me.

You love Philly.

Yeah, but they traded me.

You're familiar with the personnel there. Doug Pederson, your rookie quarterbacks coach, is back as head coach. You also know Ted Winsley, the team chaplain. Plus, you know so many great people there.

Yeah, but they traded me.

Okay, maybe I'm exaggerating a little bit. Regardless, the 2015 St. Louis trade was a mental hurdle I had to clear. Fortunately, I've got a pretty good vertical leap.

In the end, we felt drawn back to Philadelphia for a variety of reasons. In Tampa, I would only have known Coach Koetter, the former head coach at Arizona State, who I'd originally committed to my junior year of high school but never got the opportunity to play for.

But in Philadelphia, virtually everything was familiar. I also felt compelled to finish the job we'd started together in 2012: to clinch the first Super Bowl victory in franchise history. I knew my role would be different. This time I'd be assisting a talented young quarterback. Yet the chance to put on the Eagles jersey again and help Carson in his own development over the next couple of years excited me.

Ultimately, though, the biggest factor in our decision was Lily's upcoming arrival. Philly would be a familiar place, and it would provide the strong foundation and support system we'd need with a newborn on the way.

Tori and I hated to leave Kansas City. But if staying was out of the question, we couldn't imagine anyplace else we'd rather be than Philadelphia. While I would miss playing for Andy, I was excited about the prospect of reuniting with Doug Pederson. And if Carson Wentz ended up being half the player and the person Alex was, it could be a great year.

And if it wasn't?

Tori and I agreed that we'd commit to Philadelphia for two years, come what may. Then when those two years were up, we'd sit down and talk and pray about it as a couple, then follow God's lead. Stay, play, or walk away—I knew now that I could be equally content with any option.

So in March of 2017, I signed a two-year deal with the Eagles. It was official. We were returning to the City of Brotherly Love.

CHAPTER 8

BABY STEPS

A war was coming, and I knew it.

I was entering my second straight season as a backup quarterback—a condition I knew I was signing up for when I agreed to play for Philadelphia. Still, although I understood that Carson was the face of the franchise, it's human nature to want to be out on the field, making things happen.

God had done a miraculous work in my heart and reinvigorated my love of football. He had refocused my identity in Christ, and he had graciously shown me that joy and fulfillment are found not in career status, but in him.

But as the 2017 season approached, I could sense that a confrontation was brewing. For me, this fight would be a season-long inner conflict with my pride. Old habits die hard, and in my case, so did old photos.

In the heart of the NovaCare Complex, the Eagles' massive training facility near Lincoln Financial Field in South Philly, there's a hallway that extends past the media department featuring pictures of all the team's Pro Bowl players throughout the years—including a picture of me from 2013. It was a constant reminder of what was, at that point, the greatest season of my NFL career. And I was going to have to walk right past it nearly every day on my way to and from the team meeting room.

Don't get me wrong. When I signed with Philadelphia, I was genuinely excited to help Carson develop as a young quarterback. The Eagles had invested a lot of resources in him—and rightly so.

Carson had a really solid rookie year. He threw for a franchise record of 379 completions and set a single-season franchise record of 607 pass attempts, which was the second-highest by a rookie in league history. The team came out of the gate strong at 3–0 before hitting some tough patches, finishing 7–9.

I'd been the starting quarterback before. I'd been on teams that had set records, won their division, and been to the playoffs. I wanted to share the wisdom I'd gained from all those experiences. I'd also learned a lot from playing behind Alex Smith, and I figured that would be helpful to Carson as he advanced in his career. I certainly didn't have all the answers—far from it—but football is a situational game, and the more experience you have, the better prepared you are to succeed.

Coming back to Philadelphia, my mentality was *not* to eventually become the starter. I just wanted to be a stable backup. The Philly media, however, had a hard time understanding that. When I first arrived, they kept asking me, "Is this a stepping stone for you? Are you trying to become a starter again?"

When I told them no, that I just wanted to support Carson to the best of my ability, they looked at me like, *Yeah . . . he's just trying to say the right thing.* And I can see how they would think that. There's no way they could have known about my journey and why I'd decided to come back and play in the first place.

I am a competitor, so it was hard for me to stand on the sidelines. But I knew what I'd been brought to Philly to do.

If the past three seasons had taught me anything, it's that you never know what the future holds. All I wanted to do was be part of an organization that I loved and glorify God in my role, no matter what happened that season.

Unfortunately, I didn't get off to the greatest start. During training camps in July, my throwing arm started to bother me a little. As my throwing reps increased, my arm got even worse. Soon I could barely grip the ball at all. An MRI revealed that I'd developed a partial tear of a tendon in my elbow, and I ended up missing the entire preseason.

It was frustrating because I knew the majority of my snaps would come during those four games, so that would have been the optimal time for me to adjust to our new offense.

Of course, a new offense wasn't the only thing I had to adjust to that summer. Tori and I were about to experience one of the biggest changes of our lives.

WATERSHED MOMENT

The birth of a first child is a time of nervous anticipation, tender moments, and precious memories that will last a lifetime. It's also a time when grown men are apt to leave their sense of reason behind.

Our daughter, Lily, was due in mid-June, right around the end of our mandatory minicamp. Tori had stayed behind in California, since she was pregnant and couldn't travel and so she could be near her family. We still didn't have a home in Philly, and I didn't want her living in a hotel during her final few weeks. Fortunately, the team gave me their blessing to fly back home the week of mandatory minicamp so I could be with her for the final stretch.

The night Tori went into labor, I was in bed reading. We knew Lily was due to arrive any day, but Tori's words still took me by surprise.

"I think my water just broke," she called out from the bathroom.

"Are you sure?" I asked, trying to stay calm.

"I don't know. Maybe."

"Well, why don't you come to bed, then?" I suggested.

No need to panic, right?

So Tori climbed into bed, and we both went to sleep—or at least tried to.

Around 2:30 a.m., I got restless and got up to go to the bathroom. Then Tori called out from the bedroom, "Nick, get me a towel."

Without realizing that she'd gotten up and was walking toward me, I grabbed a towel and threw it across the room, accidentally nailing her right in the face. That ratcheted things up a bit.

Tori was starting to feel rushed. Me? I was perfectly calm. After all, we had prepared everything in advance. I'd seen my sisters and my sisters-in-law go through this before, so I knew labor could go on for hours.

As I walked past the closet where our hospital bags were packed, Tori said, "Where are you going?"

"I'm going to make some coffee," I said nonchalantly.

"No you're not!" she shot back. "We've got to go!"

"Tori, you're not going to have this baby for a long time. Trust me. I'll be back in five minutes. No big deal."

THE EARLY YEARS

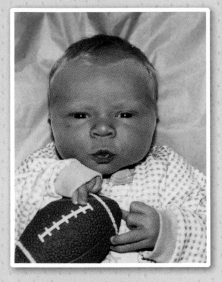

Just one day old and—thanks to my dad—already holding a football.

Me at age 10 after a particularly muddy game of Corsairs football. Not a great season, but a lot of great memories.

I don't think LeBron had anything to worry about with me, but I did earn MVP and all-district honors in basketball my sophomore and junior years at Westlake.

Westlake made it all the way to the Division I state championships my senior year. We didn't win, but I added my name to the record books for career passing yards (5,658) and touchdowns (56).

OFF TO COLLEGE

My time at MSU may have been brief, but I met a lot of great people there. Here I am with the 2007 quarterbacks team (top row: Clay Charles, John Van Dam, Brian Hoyer, Connor Dixon; bottom row: Mark Dantonio, me, Kirk Cousins, Dave Warner).

One of my most memorable games at Arizona was this win against Iowa, who was ranked in the top 10.

Celebrating Senior Day with my mom, Melissa; my dad, Larry; and my sisters, Lacey and Katie.

AND SO
IT BEGINS...

Warming up alongside
Michael Vick (#7) before a
game against the Steelers
my rookie year.

I loved playing for Andy Reid.
He was the first guy in the
NFL who really believed in
me. He gave me a chance
when nobody else would, he
saw things in me that even I
didn't know were there, and
he pushed me to do more
than I ever thought possible.

Throwing one of seven
touchdown passes I would
complete in our game against
Oakland in 2014.

Tori and me on our wedding day.

My relationship with Rams'
chaplain Mike Hansen was one
of the highlights of my season
in St. Louis. Mike encouraged
me to look for ways to have a
positive impact on my teammates
even when I wasn't starting,
and he reminded me that my
gracious response in the midst
of challenging times would be a
testimony to others.

We upset the Arizona Cardinals on the road. This was one of three touchdowns I threw that game.

INTO THE WILDERNESS

My brother-in-law Ryan and me getting ready to head off into the wilderness for a little fly-fishing in 2016. I had enough equipment to survive on Mars for a month.

That's right—I pulled this big boy out of the river all by myself. (FYI, the camera takes roughly 10 pounds and 15 inches off river trout.)

Shaking off the rust with Ryan and Evan during a late-night throwing session to get ready for training camp in Kansas City. (Not bad for a recently retired guy.)

BACK IN THE NFL

Tori and me in the tunnel at Arrowhead Stadium. She has been by my side every step of the way.

Alex Smith, Tyler Bray, and me showing off our AFC West Championship beards following our 37–27 win over the Chargers.

The 2016 season in Kansas City was a huge year for me spiritually, thanks to the support of people like Dave Meers of the KC chapter of FCA and my old friend Mike Hansen.

Our precious little girl, Lily James Foles, was born at 4:43 p.m. on June 16—incidentally, the last day of mandatory minicamp. (How many little girls can say that?)

LILY JOINS THE TEAM

Team Foles: Daddy, Mommy, Lily, and of course, our first child, Henry.

SUPER ENDING

Stepping into the end zone after catching the Philly Special. This was the first time in Super Bowl history that a quarterback both threw and caught a touchdown pass.

Lily taking a little breather on the field after the Super Bowl celebration in Minneapolis.

Me and Mickey riding the float at Disney World. I couldn't believe how many Philly fans were there that day—it was definitely magical.

With my two best girls atop the Rocky steps of the art museum after the championship parade through the streets of Philly.

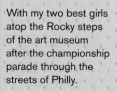

We laugh about that comment—now. At the time, though, it was about as entertaining to Tori as the anesthesiologist who ended up being a little too much of a football fan. Nothing like waiting for an epidural after eight hours of labor and having the doctor ask about your husband's football career while you're in excruciating pain.

The only thing I was a little sketchy about was watching the actual delivery. Some guys can handle it. Some can't. My dad almost passed out during all three of our births, and I was worried the same thing would happen to me.

When the time was near and the doctor asked me to help, I managed to do my part. But I was certainly glad I'd had my coffee.

Our precious little girl was born at 4:43 p.m. on June 16, the last day of mandatory minicamp. When Lily arrived, a flood of love and emotion unlike anything I'd ever felt instantly washed over me. I just stared at her in disbelief. I could hardly believe this was actually our child. After so much anticipation, it was surreal to finally meet our baby.

And for the record, I did not faint.

SETTLING IN

The rest of the 2017 off-season was a whirlwind. Not only did we have a newborn, but we also bought a home in New Jersey.

Once training camp started in late July, I moved into the Philly-area team hotel with the rest of my teammates while Tori, Lily, and Henry stayed at our off-season home in southern California. They would eventually join me on the East Coast, but first, Tori needed to get a routine established for Lily.

It was an exciting but stressful month. I was trying to get my arm back to 100 percent, and everyone was trying to be patient, but with the start of the regular season right around the corner, I also felt a lot of pressure to get back out on the field. Meanwhile, Tori and Lily were all the way across the country. Sometimes it felt more like juggling than football.

Preseason was a bit of a mixed bag. We had been hoping to win some games since the team had struggled to do so the year before. We finished 2–2, winning back-to-back games at home and losing two on the road—not exactly racking up the wins, but we were no doubt an improved team. Our passing offense, which had been twenty-second in the league the previous year, had come a long way, and Carson looked sharp, throwing for 241 yards and three touchdowns. Still, it was frustrating not being healthy enough to get out there in the mix.

Once Tori, Lily, and Henry arrived and we were able to settle into our new house as a family, things started to improve dramatically. I'd heard a lot of horror stories about babies keeping you up all night, but Lily only woke up a couple of times a night. In spite of the Bulletproof coffee genes she undoubtedly inherited from me, she was a remarkably good sleeper.

Not surprisingly, Tori transitioned into motherhood beautifully. She and Lily developed an amazing bond, and it was really cool to watch that transpire.

You might think someone in my profession would have his heart set on having a boy to throw the ball around with. And while sure, I'd love to have a son someday, I can't imagine my life without my little girl. I see so much of Tori in Lily, and I'm excited to raise a strong, confident girl. I already see a strong arm on her, and who knows— maybe she'll be a future outside hitter for the Arizona Wildcats volleyball team.

As the 2017 regular season got underway, I found myself over-whelmed by gratitude. We were adjusting to being new parents, my elbow was healthy, and we were happy to be back in the city we loved. But the wild ride was only just beginning.

CHAPTER 9

THE START OF SOMETHING SPECIAL

How do you know if a season will be magical? How do you know whether you'll finish it in utter disbelief, standing on a podium while gazing at your reflection in coveted sterling silver? How do you know if you'll be one of the few fortunate ones to be engulfed in ovations, confetti, tear-stained hugs, and a parade in front of hundreds of thousands? On that first sweltering day of training camp, how do you know how it will end more than six months later?

You don't.

You can hope for the best. You can do everything in your power to reach the promised land. But you just don't know. Each year, thirty-two teams chase the summit, but only one reaches it.

As the 2017 season opened, I felt really good about our team in Philadelphia. Granted, most players across the league feel good about their teams at the beginning of the season. September just seems to breed optimism.

Still, almost as soon as I arrived in Philadelphia, I noticed something special about my teammates. Despite the previous season's lackluster record, there was a lingering hunger from 2016. Yes, the Eagles had finished in last place in their division, and at 7–9, they were the only team in the NFC East below .500 that year. However, six of those losses were by seven points or less, and two were decided by only two points, so the prevailing sense in the locker room was that we were a lot closer to making a playoff run in 2017 than most people gave us credit for.

There are a number of factors that separate the best teams from the rest of the pack. It doesn't just mysteriously happen. All of the players in the NFL are elite athletes. Everyone—from the athletes to the coaches to the training staff—has to push themselves above and beyond if they want to be one of the last teams standing come February.

Our slogan heading into 2017 was, "Are you committed or only interested?" Everyone's *interested* in winning the Super Bowl. But it's the teams that are truly committed to it—body, mind, and soul—that actually get there. We weren't just interested. Every member of our team was 100 percent committed to winning, and you could see it from the first day of training camp. To a man, every player on our roster pushed himself every day in the weight room, in film studies, and on the practice field. Heading into 2017, we possessed a team-wide conviction unlike anything I'd seen before.

Of course, talking a big game and actually winning big games are two entirely different things. We were going to be tested right away, with back-to-back road games to start the season—first against our NFC East rival, the Redskins, and then against Andy Reid and the Chiefs, who were coming off a 12–4 season.

Nobody said the road to the Super Bowl would be easy.

AND THEY'RE OFF . . .

The season opener against the Redskins at FedEx Field was a good way to start. The whole team played well. Carson had an impressive day, throwing for 307 yards and two touchdowns, including a fifty-eight-yarder to wideout Nelson Agholor in the first quarter that Carson created by staying alive in a rapidly collapsing pocket.

Defensive tackle Fletcher Cox, who was an absolute beast all year, rounded out the scoring with a twenty-yard fumble recovery late in the fourth quarter. Our defense held Washington to a field goal in the second half, capping off a 30–17 victory.

We lost a tough one the following week to Kansas City, 27–20, and I mean a tough one. KC was up 27–13 late in the fourth; then Carson brought us to within seven on a nine-yard touchdown pass to Nelson with eight seconds left on the clock. Doug called an onside kick, which took a decidedly Philly bounce right into the waiting arms of Trey Burton on the forty-six yard line. Then, with five seconds left, Carson threw a deep ball into the end zone, where it was tipped in the air and then tumbled out of bounds as time expired. So close and yet so far. That's just how the ball bounces sometimes.

But we bounced back ourselves the following week in our home opener against the Giants. We went into the half up 7–0, courtesy of a hard-fought one-yard touchdown run by LeGarrette Blount. In the third quarter, a three-yard pass from Carson to Zach Ertz put us at 14–0. The Giants woke up in the fourth, though, scoring twenty-one unanswered points off the arm of Eli Manning. We tied it on the following drive with a fifteen-yard run from Corey Clement, but the Giants answered with a forty-one-yard field goal to retake the lead with just over three minutes left to play. That's when it became the Jake Elliott show.

We had signed Jake, a rookie place kicker, off Cincinnati's practice squad two days after the win over Washington, when Caleb Sturgis suffered a hip flexor injury in the season opener. With fifty-one seconds left in the game, Jake tied the score at 24 with a forty-six-yard field goal. Then our defense forced a three-and-out, giving us the ball back with thirteen seconds left.

Carson moved us into the outer fringes of field goal range with an incredible nineteen-yard strike to Alshon Jeffery, who caught the ball just as two defenders collided next to him. Alshon nimbly ran out of bounds with one tick left on the clock. Then Jake came onto the field for a monstrous sixty-one-yard field goal attempt to win the game. During the tense moments before the kick, Carson made a now-famous promise that was picked up by his mic: "This guy's a superhero if he makes this. . . . I'll give him my game check if he makes it."

Well, Jake nailed it. Not only that, but he set a new franchise record. We were so excited, we all ran onto the field and mobbed him. Kamu Grugier-Hill even hoisted him up in the air. And for the record, Carson made good on his promise and donated his game check to a charity of Jake's choice. Looking back, if I had to pinpoint the exact game where I first started believing this season was going to be something special, that was it.

Another sign came the following week, when we flew out to LA to take on the Chargers. We controlled the game from the get-go and ended up winning 26–24. Carson played well, throwing for 242 yards and a touchdown, and LeGarrette ran for 136. But that's not all that made it special. The real stars of that game were the fans. Eagles fans always travel well, but this was unlike anything I'd experienced before. From where I was standing, it looked like almost 80 percent of the fans in the stadium that day were ours. It was a sea of green.

It was also the first time we'd had to quiet our fans in a road game while we were on offense. When things like that happen, you know you've got something exceptional on your hands.

The following week the Cardinals came to town, and we thumped them, 34–7, putting us at a solid 4–1. That's when the momentum really started to build.

By November, Carson and our offense were really clicking. We beat the Broncos, the Cowboys, and the Bears—each by twenty-eight points—on three consecutive weeks, entering December at 10–1. Everything seemed to be going our way, and you could feel the good vibes all through the NovaCare Complex.

SUCCESS BEGINS TO BREW

Eighteen months earlier, I'd been ready to hang up my cleats. Now I had a role as Carson's backup, and I was learning to embrace it. I was excited to be in such a good environment and part of a successful team. As much as I was itching to contribute on the field, I believed God was working in me. He was showing me that it's not always about our own personal success; sometimes he calls us to play a supporting role for the people around us.

Just as I'd followed Alex's schedule in Kansas City, once I arrived in Philly, I started to get acclimated to Carson's routine. Carson liked to start early, so the whole quarterbacks team would typically get to the complex at 6 a.m. Not all of us were early birds, so this start time required the careful skill, dexterity, and commitment of a "caffeination specialist."

That would be me.

Tuesdays through Fridays, I'd make my special Bulletproof butter coffee for the three guys in our quarterbacks room and about six coaches. It was quite a process. I had to brew the coffee; put in the butter, the MCT oil, and the collagen protein; and blend the ingredients—and I had to do this three times, since I couldn't fit nine cups of coffee in the blender at once. After a while, the guys had a running joke that I must have been moonlighting as a barista somewhere.

If the coffee didn't get me going, I'd usually head over to the sports science wing and spend a few minutes "chilling out" in our cryotherapy chamber—a sauna-like contraption that uses liquid nitrogen to plunge the temperature as low as negative 260 degrees Fahrenheit to stimulate blood circulation, muscle recovery, and brain functionality. It's as uncomfortable as it sounds, but whenever I got out, I felt so much more alert and refreshed. After three minutes of deep-freezing in the cryo and a hot cup of coffee, I was ready for the day.

I loved working with Carson and with Nate Sudfeld. The three of us got along beautifully, which was a blessing since we spent the majority of our season locked away in a little ten-by-fifteen-foot room that we affectionately referred to as "the QB sanctuary."

To inject a little personality and charm into the space, Spencer Phillips, Doug Pederson's assistant, had the room wallpapered. One wall was ocean themed, and another featured a countryside scene with mountains—landscapes that clearly screamed Philadelphia. Or not. We loved it, though. For our part, we hung a few strands of white Christmas lights from the ceiling. Whenever it was time to study game film, the fluorescent overheads went off, the holiday lights came on, and *voilà!*—we had our own festive, football film–watching environment. We also had a little fridge, and of course my coffeemaker and blender were situated in one corner. A Bluetooth player allowed us to pipe in our tunes of choice—mostly Christian music and country. The room didn't inspire any HGTV spin-offs, but it got the job done.

It wasn't just the quarterback room that felt like a sanctuary; the whole locker room was like an antistress zone where anxiety couldn't find a foothold. There were just a lot of really good vibes around the complex.

Did the wins produce the good vibes, or did the good vibes play a role in helping us win? It's the chicken-or-the-egg conundrum. Personally, I think it was a mixture of both. Right from the beginning, we had a loose but disciplined team. We were structured when we needed to be, but we also felt free to relax and have a little fun when it was appropriate. Simply put, we worked hard, and we played hard.

We were also confident. There are different kinds of confidence in the NFL. Some teams exude a kind of cockiness that's easy to peg as only skin-deep. We didn't have that. We knew there was a lot of talent on our roster, and we held a genuine, well-founded belief that we could get the job done when the lights came on.

We also had a lot of faith. During my first stint with the Eagles, I was part of the team Bible study led by Ted Winsley, and I was excited to see that it was still going strong when I returned. There were a lot of strong Christians on our team that year—Carson, Zach Ertz, Trey Burton, Jordan Hicks, Chris Maragos, Stefen Wisniewski, Doug Pederson, and Frank Reich, just to name a few—and I truly believe that having that "band of brothers" to lean on made a big difference in how we carried ourselves that season. We were able to encourage each other and stay grounded, both on and off the field.

Our camaraderie was especially helpful for me. As much as I enjoyed supporting Carson and contributing to the positive vibe in the locker room, there were days I really had to fight to choose the road of humility. It wasn't always easy walking past that Pro Bowl picture every morning on my way to make coffee for Carson, Nate, and the coaching staff.

Being the team barista was a role I took on not because I had to but because I wanted to—partly because I love coffee and I knew nobody else would make it the right way, but more because it was a daily reminder to me that the best way to lead is to serve. One of my favorite Bible verses is Mark 10:45: "The Son of Man came not to be served but to serve others." I know what I've accomplished and what I'm capable of accomplishing. But the act of making coffee every morning was a daily reminder to me of who I am, who I'm here to serve, and the kind of person I want to be.

One of the other things that helped me keep my pride in check was sticking to a morning routine. Every day, I woke up, made my coffee, read Scripture for about thirty minutes, and journaled my prayers. Then, on the drive to the NovaCare Complex, I listened to Christian podcasts or music. It helped me get ready for the day and prepared my heart for whatever lay ahead. And of course, I made a habit of talking to God in prayer.

Some days were better than others, and I needed a lot of faith and strength to make it through. I was learning that walking in humility doesn't happen automatically. But it sure helped to be surrounded by such a faithful group of guys.

PHONE CALLS WITH MICKEY

In addition to the support I had in the locker room, I could also count on my family for encouragement—most notably, my grandad Mickey.

Mickey is my mom's dad. He still lives in Austin, and along with Tori and my parents, he's probably my biggest fan. At five foot seven,

Mickey was a high school track star. He ran the 4×100-meter relay at a pace that clearly did not genetically transfer to his grandson. He sacrificed much of his life to live with his mom, who needed assistance in her later years. When I was growing up, I used to love throwing the football around with him and my dad. These days he lives in a retirement home and doesn't throw anymore, but he had a great arm back in the day. I could always count on him to watch my games and cheer me on, whether I was starting or not.

Ever since I was drafted, I made it a point to call him every few weeks, just to check in with him, and that season was no exception. Every call started the same way.

"Nick, it's good to hear from you!" he would say. "Are the coaches going to let you get out there and play a little bit?"

He just couldn't understand why his grandson wasn't getting any snaps—no matter how many times I tried to explain.

"Grandad, I'm the backup quarterback. I'm not going to play. I'm there to support the starter. That's my job right now."

"Oh, okay," he'd finally concede. "Well, maybe the coach will let you play a little bit next week."

"Maybe, Grandad. Maybe."

MAN DOWN

The month of December brought with it three straight road games, including a two-game West Coast swing to Seattle and LA. When an East Coast team is scheduled to play back-to-back road games against West Coast opponents (or vice versa), the team sometimes chooses to stay in the area between games.

The decision usually comes down to team executives discussing with the sports science staff what's best for the team and what's logistically possible. Is there a good place to practice near the game site? Is it possible to fly out all our necessary equipment—for practice, for the game, and for recovery? There are a thousand details to consider. But if they can make it work, a lot of coaches prefer to do it.

NFL players are routine driven, which makes traveling tough, since it throws off your normal schedule and habits. Anytime you play on the road, especially for back-to-back weeks, it's difficult. You have to bus from your hotel to the practice site instead of driving yourself. You're not practicing at your own facility, and meetings are held in hotel conference rooms instead of your hometown training center. You're separated from your family, and you're not sleeping in your own bed at night. It just takes you out of your comfort zone.

Plus, the coaches tend to stretch out the schedule of the day's activities—partly because you're taking buses to and from practice and walk-throughs, and partly to keep you from getting distracted, especially in big cities like LA. It's football, football, football—all day, every day. On a road trip, once practice ends, I usually watch a little more film before heading back to my hotel room. Then I'll call Tori, do a devotional, read a little, and go to sleep fairly early.

Before our week fourteen game against the Rams, we practiced at Angel Stadium of Anaheim, where the Angels usually play. I have to admit, as much as I would rather have been home with Tori, Lily, and Henry, it was pretty cool. It's not often that you get to practice on a baseball diamond or hang out in an MLB locker room. But it was also a grueling week. The coaches worked us extra hard to face the Rams, who were coming into the game at 9–3 under first-year head coach Sean McVay—the franchise's best start since 2003. Adding to the stress level, Southern California had been facing some of the most destructive wildfires in state history in the weeks leading up to the game, and it definitely impacted the air quality.

This game was important on many levels. First and foremost, it pitted two division leaders against each other. With a win, we would clinch the NFC East, our first division title since 2013. On a personal level, I felt some additional pressure. There were a lot of new coaches and players on the opposing sideline this season, but even so, there's an extra tug on your heart when you face your former team.

The game started off a little wobbly, with Carson throwing an interception on the third play from scrimmage. But after that, he settled in and played one of the best games of his career. He was in complete control.

We were trailing 28–24 with 4:01 left in the third quarter when Carson led us on a long drive into the red zone. Then, on first and goal from the two yard line, Carson rolled to his right, looking for open receivers in the end zone. When he didn't see any good options, he tucked the ball and ran with it. This is where Carson excels. All season long, he'd done a fantastic job keeping plays alive with his legs—just like he did on his first scoring pass of the season, the fifty-eight-yard strike to Nelson against Washington. As he approached the end zone, he went airborne and was simultaneously met with punishing hits from linebacker Mark Barron and defensive end Morgan Fox. While he did land in the end zone, a holding penalty erased the touchdown.

Despite the hit, Carson got up quickly. But quarterbacks can read other quarterbacks pretty well, and I could tell instantly that something was wrong. I could see it in his body language and in the way he was limping. Still, he stayed in for the rest of the series and got the touchdown back on a short pass to Alshon on fourth and goal. It was Carson's thirty-third touchdown pass of the season.

As Carson came off the field, Frank Reich, our offensive coordinator and a former quarterback himself, went over to talk to Carson. Then he headed my way. "Get ready," he said. "You're probably up."

I immediately grabbed a ball and started loosening up my arm. After a few throws, Frank came back and confirmed what I'd suspected. "You're up," he said. "What would you like?"

While our defense was out on the field, Frank and I quickly reviewed the game plan and discussed the plays I wanted to run. I'd seen a little mop-up duty in our week nine and week twelve blowout wins over Denver and Chicago. But I hadn't really seen any meaningful game action in more than a year, since I started against Jacksonville the previous November in Kansas City.

I knew this was the way things work when you're the backup, but it was challenging to have my first time repping the plays with these guys come under these circumstances: in a game-time situation, on the road, in the fourth quarter. On top of that, this was a game between division leaders, with a division title on the line. And just for good measure, all of this was coming against my old team. Naturally.

When the starter goes down, though, all other factors are irrelevant. A backup has to get up to speed lightning fast—within a matter of minutes. Suddenly, you're thrust into a role you haven't been fully prepared for, and you're expected to play loose, without forcing anything, and to produce results immediately.

It's no wonder the backup often comes in and throws a pick under these conditions.

When I took the field, Jared Goff had just led the Rams on a seven-play scoring drive to take a 35–31 lead with 13:58 remaining. My goal was to keep things as simple as possible and slow everything down.

Just play ball, I told myself. *Read and react. Don't worry about making a mistake.*

On my first drive, we were able to set Jake Elliott up for a forty-one-yard field goal to bring us within one point. Then our defense came up huge. Chris Long sacked Jared Goff and forced a fumble, which safety Rodney McLeod scooped up, bringing us to another Elliott field goal and our first lead since Carson left the game.

Our defense did a fantastic job again by forcing a three-and-out on the Rams' ensuing drive, and then I made what turned out to be the play of the game for me. With 1:52 left, we were facing third and eight at our own twenty-three yard line. It was a crucial moment. If we got the first down, we could run out the clock and win the game. If we didn't get the first down, the Rams would get the ball back with great field position and plenty of time to win it with a field goal.

The play we ran was designed as a passing play to Alshon, who was on my left. They'd been singling up on Alshon all day, which is why Doug called the play. But once we lined up, they went into a cover two man package, where two safeties play deep and another defensive back provides man-to-man coverage to take away inside leverage. It was the same play that had resulted in an interception early in the game.

This defense took away Alshon's route, which meant my only remaining option was Nelson Agholor, who was running a slot lightning route—also known as an eight-yard stop route. He would have to run the route a hair deeper because it was third and eight, and for the play to work, he would have to break down and away. My throw would also have to be delivered with pinpoint accuracy.

It all played out as planned. I threw a perfect pass, and Nelson made a great catch, securing a first down. A few downs later, on the Rams' final desperation play, Brandon Graham scooped up a fumble recovery and rumbled sixteen yards into the end zone to bring the final score to 43–35.

We came off the field feeling great about the victory, but our minds quickly switched back to Carson. The win had come at a high cost. At that point, we didn't know the extent of his injury, but all of us were concerned.

The first thing I wanted to do was get to the locker room and find out how Carson was. Being a backup is an awkward role, in that your success is ultimately predicated on someone else's tragedy. That said, you never want to see anyone get hurt—especially a good friend like Carson. Whenever a player goes down on the field—whether it's one of my teammates or the opposition—my first instinct is to pray that they'll be okay. My second instinct is to put it behind me, focus, and do my job. That afternoon, I had to do both.

In the locker room, I could tell Carson was hurting. He did his best to mask it, greeting and congratulating each of us as we came in, but the pain was obvious in his eyes. Although the MRI of his knee wasn't scheduled until the following morning, he seemed resigned to the idea that his season was probably over.

The plane ride home was tough. Winning the NFC East was a big deal, and everyone was excited. But our enthusiasm was tempered by the knowledge that our starting quarterback had suffered a potentially serious injury. In addition to being one of the leaders of our team, Carson was also a front-runner for the league MVP award. A loss like that wouldn't be easy for any team to overcome.

I typically don't sleep much on flights home after games, and this one was no exception. After sitting there thinking for a while, I pulled up some video of the Rams game on my iPad, watched a TV show, and listened to some music. But then my mind started to drift ahead to the coming days.

As our plane cruised along at 35,000 feet, my thoughts and emotions began to swirl. I was genuinely hurting for Carson. I knew what it felt like to suffer a season-ending injury, and I wouldn't wish that on anyone. Based on the team doctor's preliminary diagnosis and the amount of discomfort Carson was in, I was already getting mentally prepared to finish the rest of the season.

It was a strange limbo to be caught in. On the one hand, I needed to prepare myself mentally to lead the team. But on the other hand, I was hoping for the best—that Carson's MRI results would indicate things weren't as serious as we feared and that he'd be ready to roll in time for the playoffs.

Questions began racing through my mind. Would I be able to get up to speed quickly enough? After standing on the sidelines all season, what kind of level would I be able to play at? How would fans and the media react to the idea of Carson being gone and my stepping in at such a critical juncture? Would I be able to tune out all the outside noise and distractions and focus on the task at hand? What if I couldn't? Then again, what if I could?

I thought back to everything I'd been through emotionally and spiritually over the past few years—getting traded from Philly, being benched in St. Louis, flirting with retirement, then coming back. I thought about the limited reps I'd received that season—first in the preseason because of my elbow injury, and then in the regular season as I ran the scout team. And now I had three games to get ready for the playoffs. The division title was in hand, but we still had plenty of goals ahead of us as a team: to get a first-round bye, to have home-field advantage throughout the postseason, and of course, the big one—the goal every team strives for each year, but only one attains—winning it all.

The future was hazy. But as we made our way back to the East Coast in the early hours of the morning, I could feel time slipping away. I had a huge task to accomplish and not long to prepare for it. I knew I had to slow everything down and try not to look too far ahead, but it wasn't going to be easy. Then again, nothing worthwhile ever is.

The next day was technically an off day, but not for me. I would go in, do my normal Monday prep work, and keep the weekly schedule the same as always. I had a routine I was comfortable with, and I intended to stick with it so I'd be prepared come game time. This helped provide a little peace of mind in the midst of the growing chaos.

Because make no mistake, chaos *was* coming.

CHAPTER 10

THIRTEEN AND THREE

When I walked into our house ten hours later, Lily and Henry were snoozing. Tori was in bed, though not fully asleep. I was exhausted, but how could I go right to sleep after what had happened, knowing what might lie ahead? Tori and I talked for a little while, processing what had happened to Carson and how much we were both hurting for him. Then we talked about the possible challenges ahead before drifting off to sleep.

I arrived at the facility early Monday, as usual, and got to work prepping for our next game, against the Giants. Later that morning, I saw Carson sitting on a table in the training room with a brace on his knee. That's when he broke the news to me—his season was over. The MRI revealed that his knee was pretty torn up and would require surgery and significant rehabilitation. He handled it well, but I suspected he was dealing with a whirlwind of emotions. I'd suffered season-ending injuries before, but never under these circumstances—having just led my team into the playoffs, and in contention for league MVP. I could only imagine how this made him feel.

After I finished my work for the day, I picked up Tori and Lily and took them out to lunch at a local burrito bar near our house in New Jersey. With my hat on, I was able to remain fairly inconspicuous, which turned out to be a blessing, because as soon as we sat down, we overheard the following conversation at the table next to us.

"Did you hear what happened to Carson Wentz? He's out for the season."

"Well, I guess we'll just have to wait another year for the Super Bowl."

Tori and I just looked at each other and kept eating.

I don't think people doubted that I could play, but a Super Bowl run? It seemed like a long shot. And why wouldn't it be? In a city that had never won a Super Bowl, who would believe that a guy who had played only a handful of snaps all season could come in at the end of the season and lead the team to a championship?

There's a reason franchise quarterbacks command such high salaries. The backup isn't usually *the guy*, so people tend to doubt their ability to do big things. From a fan's perspective, the odds weren't in our favor, and I couldn't blame them for being skeptical.

But inside the NovaCare Complex, there was never any doubt. The team knew I had experience playing in—and winning—big games. After all, I wasn't a rookie. I was a seasoned veteran with a record-setting season and a Pro Bowl under my belt. And the support I received from everyone in the organization reflected that.

Of course, we still had work to do. We would have to put in a lot of extra practice to get my timing down with our receivers. They'd established a strong rhythm with Carson, but Alshon Jeffery,

Nelson Agholor, Torrey Smith, and Mack Hollins were all new to me. I already had great relationships with Zach Ertz, Brent Celek, and Trey Burton from my previous stint in Philadelphia, so that was one part we didn't have to create from scratch. Still, it was a huge task—and the stakes were high.

It wasn't long before the texts and calls began to roll in on Tori's phone. Everyone wanted to find out what was happening. It was a lot to process—and a lot had changed practically overnight. As we acclimated to our new reality, we talked and prayed and leaned on each other in deeper ways than we had before. I was grateful that we could be transparent about all the emotion and stress that kept crashing over us in waves. We didn't want anxiety or fear to have any power in our lives, and maintaining open communication was a big part of winning that battle.

We also made it a priority to keep our weekly date night on the schedule. It was important for us to get out of the house for a couple of hours and focus on our relationship. With all the craziness surrounding us, we needed that time to stay grounded.

Tori is an amazingly strong woman. It's a good thing too, because she needed every bit as much grace and strength as I did during that time. The Bible says that in marriage, a husband and wife "are united into one" (Genesis 2:24), and we were experiencing that reality in a new way. My joy was Tori's joy. My pain was her pain. And vice versa. When I became the Eagles' starter, she carried my hopes and burdens in a way no one else could, all while doing the vital work of being a wife and a mom and taking care of our household.

Anxiety crept in at times, but whenever it did, we turned to the Lord through prayer and reading his Word. In the midst of everything that was going on around us—and in many ways, because of it—our faith was growing by leaps and bounds.

HURRY-UP OFFENSE

Professional football has a nasty habit of desensitizing you. It's such a fast-paced, results-driven sport, and players come and go so frequently that it's easy to forget about the personal side of it. The best way I know to avoid that dehumanizing process is to forge deep bonds with my teammates. When one of my brothers on the team is hurting, I hurt too.

But another harsh NFL reality is that you don't have a lot of time to sit with the pain. The schedule surges forward, no matter what. Come next weekend, there's always another game. You can't remain stagnant; you have to move on—adjusting, learning, and growing as you go.

After Carson's injury, the local media began questioning me about taking over as the starter. I imagine that most of them figured I would say something to the effect of, "This is my team now." If so, they figured wrong. This was still Carson's team. He was still the starting quarterback, and I said as much in those initial interviews.

The media was surprised. They prodded me, suggesting that at some point I would eventually have to adopt the "this is my team" mentality.

I disagreed. I didn't have to have ownership to go out there and play at a high level. I would play my guts out every game, but that didn't change the fact that I knew Carson's role and I knew my role.

Three days after the injury, Carson was in Pittsburgh for reconstructive knee surgery. Afterward, he had to face a great deal of pain, not to mention all the questions and emotions. He handled himself with class, although it couldn't have been easy. When you've been performing at an elite level—both personally and as a team—it's hard to suddenly be sidelined by circumstances outside your control.

About two weeks later, after he'd regained at least a little mobility in his leg, Carson began showing up in the impeccably decorated QB sanctuary for morning film sessions with Nate and me. He wanted to help the team in any way he could.

In many ways, this was a complete role reversal for someone in his position. When you're the starter, you dictate what time the meeting begins and how the meeting flows, and you're completely focused on what you have to do to prepare to play the upcoming opponent. But when Carson returned to our meetings, he took on a supportive role. That's not an easy transition—believe me; I know—but he handled everything with an impressive amount of humility, grace, and maturity.

One thing that impressed me was how he continued to stay locked in on what we were doing and kept processing the game plan even after it was clear that he was out. When we were reviewing film, he would share his ideas for different plays, and he knew what we wanted to do for each game—what the plays were, all the details. That spoke volumes about his character and his love for the team, especially given the intense rehab process he had to endure.

Of course, Carson wasn't the only one going through a difficult transition. The whole team had a monumental challenge in front of us as we tried to adapt after losing our MVP-caliber starting quarterback. There's no manual for that. You just have to figure it out as you go.

The faith my teammates showed in me during this transition was inspiring. Many of them had played with me during my first stint with Philly—guys like Brent, Zach, Trey, Lane Johnson, Donnie Jones, and Jason Kelce. They had seen what I'd accomplished earlier in my career, and I think that familiarity gave them a lot of confidence.

The big question was, could I pick up the speed of the game in time for the postseason? The guys had faith in me, but we all knew the learning curve would be steep. After all, I'd missed the entire preseason and thrown a total of four live passes before the game in Los Angeles. Growing pains would be inevitable.

All season long, the offense had been predicated on Carson and his skill set. Now, in less time than it takes to snap a ball, everything had changed. We had to recalibrate the offense based on what was comfortable for me, and we had only three regular-season games left to do it.

Doug Pederson, Frank Reich, John DeFilippo, Press Taylor, Spencer Phillips, Duce Staley, and Jeff Stoutland all stepped in to improvise, working to build an offense around me as quickly as possible. We had several goals: make a game plan for each week's opponent, try to earn the top playoff seeding, and strategize for home-field advantage.

While the coaches were shifting some of their strategies to maximize my comfort, I was trying to get comfortable in my new role. It was a bit disorienting to step into the starting huddle again and execute the plays with guys I'd never repped with before. The fact that my transition happened during the holiday season didn't make things any easier. That whole period was like a mad science experiment.

I'm sure a lot of folks were wondering, *Can Nick get up to speed this fast?* And I don't blame them for thinking that. Quite frankly, I was wondering the same thing.

One afternoon Nate and I were heading back from the weight room, and we passed my Pro Bowl picture hanging on the wall. I walked by the picture, slapped the wall, and said, "About time for you to come back."

We both had a good laugh, but make no mistake: I was well aware of the realities we were facing. I'd spent most of the season on the sideline, and now I was supposed to instantly get up to NFL game speed, finish the season strong, make a run through the playoffs, and lead this team to the Super Bowl?

From a human standpoint, all that was pretty impossible. If I had any hope of meeting those goals, it would only be by God's grace. And I'm not throwing out that phrase tritely. It was the truth. I serve a God for whom nothing is impossible, and I was surrounded by an amazing group of coaches, players, and support staff, all of whom were as dedicated to achieving those goals as I was.

When Carson got injured, the national and local media outlets, social media, and even lunchtime patrons in South Jersey burrito joints changed their predictions for our season. One minute everyone was anointing us as a Super Bowl favorite; the next, the chatter had turned to doom and gloom. We had only changed the position of one player, but that was enough to turn us into the underdog.

What many outsiders forgot in the immediate aftermath of the Rams game was the talent, commitment, and character that remained on the team. We still had a skilled, highly motivated group of guys who were ready to prove we could overcome a loss even as significant as losing our quarterback. Our first task? Travel ninety minutes north on Interstate 95 to face the Giants.

SLAYING THE GIANTS

When we came into town, the Giants were sitting at 2–11, their worst season since 1974. The team was enduring a lot of internal upheaval too, with the firing of head coach Ben McAdoo and general manager Jerry Reese two weeks earlier, after Eli Manning was benched and the team fell to Oakland 24–17.

But if you know anything about NFC East football, the old axiom holds true: records don't mean anything when division rivals meet. Plus Manning was back under center, and despite the Giants' record that season, he was still an extremely talented and dangerous quarterback who already owned two Super Bowl rings. The fact that he was coming off of a highly controversial benching that ended his potentially record-setting consecutive-games streak meant he was going to be playing with something to prove.

Well, so were we.

As expected, Manning came out of the gate like a bullet, running thirteen straight no-huddle plays and driving seventy-five yards downfield for a touchdown. But we answered. First our defense blocked the extra point to hold the Giants to six. Then in my first starting drive in fourteen months, I went three for four, then hit Alshon Jeffrey on a back endline route in the back of the end zone to tie it up, and the extra point gave us an early lead.

We lost the lead on the next drive when Manning hit Tavarres King for a thirteen-yard touchdown play at the end of the first quarter, then found Sterling Shepard for a sixty-seven-yard catch-and-run on the next series.

Midway through the second quarter, we were down 20–7, and the Giants were driving again when Ronald Darby intercepted a pass intended for Roger Lewis and returned it thirty-seven yards, setting us up on the Giants' twenty. The Giants brought a cover zero blitz, and I connected with Zach Ertz over the middle for a touchdown.

Our defense came up big on the next series, sacking Manning for a loss of five and then blocking a punt, giving us another short field inside the twenty. Then, on a third and five, the Giants busted their coverage, and I hit Trey Burton on a slot fade route to retake the lead.

After we exchanged field goals, I threw a jump ball to Nelson

Agholor, who outleaped Darryl Morris to pull down the touchdown, putting us up 31–23.

Late in the third, Manning and Tavarres King hooked up for their second touchdown of the day, this time for fifty-seven yards, bringing the Giants within two.

That's when our defense came up big yet again, sacking Manning and foiling the Giants' two-point conversion attempt.

Jake nailed a twenty-yard field goal late in the fourth to give us a five-point cushion, and then our defense stopped the Giants' final two drives to secure the win and a first-round bye.

It was a hard-fought victory. By the time the clock ran out, Eli Manning and I had both posted season-high passing games. He went thirty-seven for fifty-seven and 434 yards with three touchdowns, and I went twenty-four for thirty-eight and 237 yards with four touchdowns.

Not bad for a guy who hadn't played a full game in over a year.

BLACK AND BLUE CHRISTMAS

The following week, we had a game on Christmas Day against Oakland. It was my first start against the Raiders since my seven-touchdown performance in 2013. However, there would be no offensive fireworks this time around. The thermometer read twenty-nine degrees at kickoff, and with a fifteen-mile-per-hour wind, it felt even colder.

Late in the first quarter, I connected on a screen pass with running back Jay Ajayi, our midseason pickup from the Dolphins, for a seventeen-yard touchdown. That would turn out to be my only scoring pass of the game.

Near the end of the game, I was missing throws that I should have been hitting in my sleep. Yet we still had an opportunity to win. With just under a minute left, Ronald Darby, who had intercepted Eli Manning the previous week, set us up with another huge defensive play, this time intercepting Derek Carr near midfield.

I completed four of five passes to get us to the Raiders' thirty-one yard line, where Jake drilled a forty-eight-yard field goal. A few seconds later, as Oakland was trying to lateral their way down the field, defensive end Derek Barnett capped the game with a twenty-three-yard fumble return for a touchdown.

We won with a score of 19–10 and clinched home-field advantage throughout the playoffs, but the media still had a field day with our offensive struggles. My four-touchdown performance against the Giants the week before was suddenly dubbed a fluke, and sportswriters across the league declared that the "real Nick" was starting to show his true colors.

It's moments like these when I'm especially grateful for my support system.

"You are the most dangerous player in the world right now," my dad told me. "When everyone doubts you, that's when you come to life and really light things up."

My dad's encouragement in that moment meant a lot to me. It was nice to know that even though the media had stopped believing in me, the people closest to me knew that I was capable of winning.

There's no sugarcoating it: I didn't play well in the Oakland game. I was thinking too much. I was trying to play the offense too perfectly instead of just letting it rip.

It's not easy to pull yourself out of a funk like that. But with faith and perseverance, it can happen. When I start to overthink things or doubt myself, I have to get out of my own head and stop trying to fix the problem on my own. I need to remember that God has given me my abilities and that I'm here to glorify him. This perspective helps me relax and slows the game down a little.

So what does that look like? When things are going poorly, I take a moment and gather my thoughts, say a prayer, and remind myself not to take everything so seriously. Sometimes I'll even give myself a little pep talk, like, *Wow, you're really stinking it up out here today. But it's not the end of the world. You can get out of this. Just stop being so serious. Go sling the ball and have some fun.*

Inevitably, when I'm having a bad game, people will come up to me on the sidelines and offer their support. But when it comes right down to it, they can only offer advice and solidarity. No one else can do it for you. You have to make the change yourself. For me, that means believing God is capable of using me to do great things if I lean on him.

When the media covered the Oakland game, they mostly focused on how poorly I had played. But honestly, that was one of my all-time favorite games—not just because it clinched the home-field advantage for us, but because of how well we responded to adversity as a team. You're not going to score forty points every week. Some games you have to scrape and claw for every last yard. It says a lot about a team when you win that type of game, and I was really proud of how our guys stuck together and continued to play hard the entire sixty minutes.

Although the scoreboard didn't reflect it, our offense showed a tremendous amount of grit against Oakland. And our defense did a great job keeping us in the game so we could have the opportunity we needed at the end. I don't care what the media says; an ugly win is better than a pretty loss any day. Interestingly enough, the Raiders' late owner Al Davis was famous for saying, "Just win, baby!" I suppose we took a page from his playbook that Christmas and did just that.

GOING OUT WITH A CLANG

We went into our final regular-season game against Dallas on New Year's Eve with absolutely nothing to lose—except, of course, the game.

The game itself was a bitterly cold slog. Neither team could get anything going on offense for most of the afternoon. In fact, it was the first NFL game to be 0–0 at halftime since week fourteen of 2011, when the Bears and the Broncos failed to convert on any of their first-half drives.

The Cowboys scored the game's only points when quarterback Dak Prescott threw a twenty-yard touchdown pass early in the fourth quarter. In keeping with the day's theme, they then missed the extra point. All told, both teams combined for three turnovers and a 27 percent conversion rate on third downs. Suffice it to say, it wasn't pretty.

I played the entire first quarter, throwing for a whopping thirty-nine yards and one interception and racking up a deplorable 9.3 quarterback rating before I gave way for Nate. As ugly as things looked, we were sticking with our original plan. Our playoff picture wasn't going to change whether we won or lost, and the coaching staff didn't want to risk any injuries heading into the postseason.

That said, our pride sure took a beating. You always want to play well and win, but practically speaking, it becomes a question of opportunity cost. Is it worth winning a meaningless game if, in the process, you end up losing one or more key players heading into the playoffs? History would dictate no, even if it meant giving the media one more reason to call our competence into question.

Losing to our fiercest division rival was certainly not an ideal way to end the regular season. But as we took a step back and considered what we had accomplished, it was still satisfying. Entering the play-offs, we were the top seed in the NFC at 13–3, with home-field advantage throughout, which meant that the road to the Super Bowl was going to come through Philadelphia.

That was a huge accomplishment. There's only one team in recent history that has made a habit of winning twelve or thirteen games a year, and our paths would cross soon enough. But as a general rule, a 13–3 season is extremely difficult to accomplish. Take the Eagles' division, the NFC East, for example. Since winning Super Bowl XXVII after the 1992 season, Dallas has done it only twice (2007 and 2016). Not even in their championship seasons of 1993 and 1995 did they reach thirteen regular-season wins (they went 12–4 both years).

Bill Parcells led the Giants to a 14–2 season in 1986 and a 13–3 mark in 1990 en route to two Super Bowl victories, but New York hasn't accomplished the feat since. And the Redskins are in a similar spot. They have to dip back into the Joe Gibbs glory days of 1983 and 1991—both 14–2 regular seasons that ended in Super Bowl appearances—to find such lofty regular-season win totals.

As for the Eagles, prior to 2017, the franchise had achieved thir-teen wins only once before in its long history, when Andy Reid and Donovan McNabb led the 2004 team to a 13–3 record and Super Bowl XXXIX, where they fell just short against New England.

So we were extremely pleased with a 13–3 season, especially when you consider that all three of our losses came against teams that ended the season with winning records (Kansas City, Seattle, and Dallas), two of those games were on the road, and one saw most of our starters standing on the sidelines. And we weren't done yet.

The media, however, didn't view it that way. Our less-than-impressive performances against Dallas and Oakland precipitated an avalanche of criticism and doubt. It was hard to find anyone in the sports world who believed we were a real postseason threat anymore. You could even see it reflected in the playoff betting odds. I mean, when was the last time a conference champion was a playoff underdog at home for two straight weeks?

Negativity is a reality we all have to contend with. Most people aren't wired to see the best in people; we're more likely to complain, point the finger, and pass judgment. This isn't unique to the world of sports—it's simply human nature. Only by God's grace does kindness enter the picture.

So it didn't come as a surprise to me when the media attacked, when social media blew up, and when people expressed doubt in us. Unfortunately, knowing the criticism is coming doesn't make it any easier to deal with. I never watch sports commentary or read the newspaper or listen to sports talk radio. Even so, as the regular season drew to a close, I knew what everyone was saying about me—and about the Eagles' playoff chances with me as the starting quarterback. It was obvious from the tenor of questions during my press conferences each week.

All season long, the media had been saying good things about us. Now I constantly got questions about my poor performances, and I tried my best to answer each question respectfully. Fortunately, I've developed a fairly thick skin over the years, and that helps with handling criticism. Even so, for the good of the team and my own ability to focus, I had to draw a line. So I said to Tori and my family, "Don't tell me anything you hear or read about me." Once that negative feedback gets in your head, it affects you, and I needed my mind to be as clear as possible heading into the playoffs. I believed in my teammates and my coaches, and I knew we'd eventually find a rhythm.

The toughest part was watching my family process all the comments about me—how I was failing the team and how I was going to cause an early playoff exit. I might have been the one physically playing the game, but my family lives and dies every single play with me. I knew how frustrating it was for Tori and my parents to read the negative press, and that was difficult for me to bear.

In the meantime, our home became a place of solace for me. As soon as I walked through the front door each night, I found a safe harbor in the midst of the storm.

My first order of business after practice was to spend time with Lily. It gave me so much joy to look into her sweet, innocent face and realize that, at six and a half months old, she didn't have the slightest idea what was happening with my career. She didn't care what my quarterback rating was or how many picks I threw against Dallas. She just wanted to be held by Daddy—and to dance with him to Ed Sheeran.

Lily loves two songs in particular by the British singer—"Galway Girl" and "Perfect"—so every night near the end of the season, I'd play those music videos, and we'd have a little family dance party. I'd scoop Lily into my arms, and Tori would grab Henry, and we'd all have a ball dancing to Ed. It was our way to cut loose and have fun as a family before Lily's bedtime. And it was the perfect way for me to relax, recalibrate, and remind myself of what was really important.

Once Lily was asleep, I'd take a thirty-minute Epsom salt bath to recover from the day and process my thoughts. Then as we got ready for bed, Tori and I would talk about the pressure I was facing and how we were processing everything. We tried to lift our eyes off the details and consider the big picture, while also not peering too far down the road. Philippians 4:6-7 says, "Don't worry about anything; instead, pray about everything. Tell God what you need, and thank him for all he has done. Then you will experience God's peace, which exceeds anything we can understand. His peace will guard your hearts and minds as you live in Christ Jesus." That's what we tried to do.

Those nightly conversations with Tori were therapeutic for me. Instead of giving in to doubt and fear, we stuck together and became stronger in the process. It may have been a stressful time in my career, but it was also a wonderful time of growth and unity in our marriage.

By 9 p.m., my head would hit the pillow. Everything would start up again when the alarm went off at 4:45 a.m.

The regular season was officially over. Playoffs loomed ahead.

Once again I found myself thinking about the guy in the Pro Bowl photo at the NovaCare Complex. *Man, I hope that guy comes back soon.*

CHAPTER 11

HOME-FIELD ADVANTAGE

Professional football is a game of power, speed, and extraordinary athletic feats. But during one of the most pivotal weeks of my career, I was seated on my backside staring at a flickering screen.

When I woke up on January 1, 2018, our 6–0 loss to Dallas was in the rearview mirror and an NFC divisional-round playoff game was just twelve days away. Our opponent would be determined by the wild-card games occurring during the weekend of January 6–7.

As the NFC's top seed, we enjoyed a first-round playoff bye, but that didn't mean I was spending that first week of January out on the golf course or jetting to the Caribbean. On the contrary, we saw that extra week as a chance to dig into the film archives and watch some of my old games from my first stint with Philadelphia. For several hours that week, I parked myself in the QB sanctuary and watched video of my best throws as an Eagle in 2013 and 2014.

This wasn't a nostalgia tour or an exercise in vanity. I had a very specific agenda: to pinpoint how I had achieved the greatest success of my career and find a way to replicate the comfort level I'd experienced then. Not only would it be a great confidence boost, but it would help Doug, Frank, and the others compile a game plan that I could thrive in. It can be difficult for backups to find their stride since the offense isn't designed for them, so I was grateful for the chance to build something new around my style.

When NFL coaches or players talk about watching film, it's a much more involved process than sitting back with a bag of chips and watching TV. In every position room in a team training facility—the quarterbacks room, the running backs room, the receivers room—there's a computer where the team's video department keeps a massive database of all the games in the NFL. The videos include a backside view for the interior linemen as well as a widescreen view so you can see the route concepts and get the full picture for each play. Depending on the type of offense or defense you're playing against the following week, coaches can ask the video department to create a compilation of all of the plays that apply to a particular scheme. They can also break it down by season, team, or play type—or even individual players. So you're not rewatching an entire game but rather compilations of specific plays recorded from a variety of different angles.

In my case, Frank had asked the video department to create a couple of cut-ups, as we call them, that highlighted all my passing completions for fifteen yards or more from 2013 and 2014. There were about 150 over the course of those two seasons. That week I reviewed my complete 150 cut-up, as well as a highlight cut-up featuring the plays I liked from those 150.

As I watched the film, something immediately stuck out to me:

I wasn't just taking the snap, doing a five-step drop, and throwing downfield; I was moving in the pocket, scrambling outside it, and throwing the ball with different arm angles—sometimes over the top and sometimes with a quick flick of the wrist. I was playing basketball on the football field, and it was pure joy to behold.

There in that cramped room decorated with all the style of men who play a contact sport for a living, the seeds of a new beginning began to take root. I began to rediscover who I truly was as a quarterback.

Watching that film also reinforced my longstanding belief that I perform my best when I'm reading the situation and reacting to it—just playing ball, not overthinking things. Some quarterbacks prefer to think through everything and tick through a mental checklist on each play. Not me. I need to keep things simple. My strength is in reacting and going with my gut. It's always been this way—all the way back to my days at Westlake, when defensive coverages were as foreign to me as Michigan snowstorms and I played on pure instinct.

Since then, I've learned the full gamut of coverages and blitz packages. But as I watched myself in those highlight reels, it was almost like being in a time warp—seeing myself in 2013 and 2014 onscreen, but also seeing shadows of my prep days in Texas. I could see where I'd been, as well as how my past experiences could help me get to where I wanted to go.

My tendency to play by instinct doesn't mean that I don't study or that I ignore the fundamentals. In fact, it's just the opposite. When I'm in the film room or at quarterback meetings, I take notes and soak up as much knowledge as I possibly can. I want to know every detail on how various plays are designed, why we're running them, and what we're looking for. If I'm going to achieve optimum performance on the field, I need to do a ton of thinking in the film and meeting rooms to ingrain our offensive schemes into my brain. That way, when I run the play during a game, it's already instinctual, and I won't have to expend time and energy grinding my mental gears. That's the happy medium I look for—learning and thinking during practice, then trusting my gut when I play.

With the Rams, I was running an offense designed for anyone, not one specific to me. Now, however, Doug, Frank, and the rest of the coaching staff were molding the offense around my individual strengths. That took a lot of pressure off me.

In addition to the film studies, we were doing two full-steam-ahead practices that week—first-team offense vs. first-team defense—and we just played ball. The coaching staff gave us scripted plays to run, but because we still had no idea who we would be playing, we weren't following a specific game plan. Essentially, we were running plays that I liked and scrimmaging against our defense at full speed.

The coaches wanted me to get back to playing the way I used to—free and loose. Too much focus on fundamentals and mechanics had slowed me down. I needed to trust my instincts and not just stand in for Carson, but play *my* game at a high level. That was the key that week: just play. There was no reason to try to become someone I'm not. I'd fallen into that trap several times in my career—and never seen positive results.

Don't worry about anything, I kept telling myself during practice that week. *Just read and react and let it rip!*

Because the coaches allowed me to play freely, I was able to get into a rhythm. I felt like myself again, and everything was clicking. I started to believe I could make any throw I needed to.

Of course, feeling confident in the film room and on the practice field is one thing. Playing well in front of nearly seventy thousand screaming fans in the playoffs is another.

That Saturday, Atlanta defeated the Rams 26–13. The Falcons were coming to town with one of the best defenses in football. The fact that the Falcons were looking for redemption after blowing a twenty-five-point lead to New England in Super Bowl LI was not lost on anyone in our locker room. We knew we were in for a dogfight.

EVERY DOG HAS ITS DAY

Going into the Falcons game, Las Vegas had us as the 2.5-point underdogs at home. It was the first time bookmakers had not favored a number one seed to win its first playoff game since the NFL's postseason format expanded to twelve teams back in 1990.

Yeah. We didn't like that very much.

When we fell one game short of making the playoffs in 2014 and I was traded to the Rams, I never thought I'd get the opportunity to play in a postseason game in Philly. The fact that I was able to put on an Eagles jersey again three years later and return to do just that was something that I didn't deserve, but I was so grateful to get the chance.

Favored or not, come game day, we knew that Lincoln Financial Field (or the Linc) would be sold out. The atmosphere around the stadium was bound to be electric, and the Philly faithful would be loud and rowdy. It's no wonder we played so well at home—especially on defense.

Speaking of defense, Atlanta's was top notch, but not unbeatable. You just have to take what they give you. For example, the Falcons' defense allows for a lot of completions underneath the coverage. They don't want to get beat deep—they want to keep everything in front of them and rally to the ball. Typically they play post safety zone coverage, but they like to mix it up with post safety man coverage. It's basically the Seattle defense. Atlanta's head coach, Dan Quinn, was the defensive coordinator in Seattle during their consecutive Super Bowl appearances during the 2013 and 2014 seasons, and he brought a lot of those concepts with him. We were going to execute our offense and run the ball well. I would go through my progression and play smart but aggressive.

By the time kickoff arrived, we expected it to be cold, but we didn't expect the winds to be quite as gusty as they were. Throwing with a nasty wind makes things difficult for a passer. Even when the wind is at your back, it can play havoc with longer passes. Kickers don't especially care for it either. And as it turned out, a good portion of this game would ride on the leg of Jake Elliott.

On our opening drive, we were throwing into the wind, but I decided to go ahead and test the waters with a double-move route to Torrey Smith. The ball had a little wobble to it initially, and the wind ate it up, causing it to fall short. However, Torrey got tangled up with two Atlanta defenders on the play, which resulted in a pass interference and a forty-two-yard gain. Unfortunately, on the next play we fumbled the ball, and Atlanta recovered. Matt Ryan engineered a ten-play drive back down the field, where our defense held them to a field goal. That series pretty much characterized the entire game—big plays, the occasional bobble, defensive stands, and field goals.

As a case in point, early in the second quarter, Nelson Agholor ran around the line and made a spectacular twenty-one-yard run before getting forced out of bounds at the three. Then we handed off the ball, but it got stripped. I dove on it and stretched into the end zone for a touchdown. A few seconds later, the touchdown call was reversed when it was determined that Atlanta's Brian Poole had landed on my legs before the ball crossed the plane. That put us at fourth and one from the one, and in his first gut-check call of the postseason, Doug decided to go for it. We went right back to LeGarrette, who ran wide right, held off a defender, and went straight into the end zone to put us up 6–3.

A few minutes later, Atlanta punted the ball into the wind, and it dropped right into the middle of a scrum. From there it took a sideways bounce, ricocheted off three of our guys, and then was picked up by Atlanta's LaRoy Reynolds inside the red zone. Four plays later, Matt Ryan hit Devonta Freeman in the end zone, putting Atlanta up 10–6.

But the wild bounces didn't stop there. Late in the second quarter, Fletcher Cox absolutely flattened Matt Ryan, forcing a punt with less than a minute remaining in the half. Then Bryan Braman tipped the ball as it was coming off Matt Bosher's foot, stalling the punt at the twenty-eight yard line. On the next play, I got hit in the legs just as I was about to throw, and the ball ended up sailing right over Zach Ertz's head and straight toward Atlanta's Keanu Neal. I thought for sure it was going to be a pick, but somehow it ended up ricocheting off Neal's right knee and shooting ten yards the other way, right into the arms of Torrey Smith. Torrey pulled it in and ran it back to the fifty, where a stunned Keanu was waiting to bring him down. With less than six seconds left to play, I hit Alshon Jeffery on a fifteen-yard connect route to the right, and he managed to step out of bounds at the thirty-five with one second left, setting Jake up for a massive fifty-three-yard field goal. He just nailed that ball—and into the wind, no less.

During the second half, the rhythm really started to flow for me. I didn't throw any touchdown passes, but I didn't have any interceptions either, and we engineered two long drives that burned a lot of time off the clock. That gave our defense a chance to rest and set Jake up for two more field goals.

Ryan kept things interesting right up until the end, and our defense made a fantastic last stand in the closing minute of the game. On fourth and goal, with less than fifteen seconds on the clock, Ryan tossed a final floater into the end zone that ended up sailing through the hands of Julio Jones, giving us the ball back and sealing the victory at 15–10.

All told, I completed twenty-three of thirty attempts for 246 yards. But there's no question this was a team win all the way. It felt great to get into a rhythm and to beat an outstanding opponent. This was a win we could really build off of.

After the game, a couple of my teammates, Lane Johnson and Chris Long, put on rubber dog masks while conducting postgame interviews. It was a playful poke at our underdog status, and practically overnight, it became a Philly fan phenomenon. By the time we took the field again the following week, there would be thousands of dog masks staring back at us from the stands.

We were now just one win away from the Super Bowl, and the excitement around Philly was amplifying. So was the level of difficulty.

Next up: the Minnesota Vikings.

FLYING PURPLE PEOPLE EATERS

It's hard to exaggerate the magnitude of the NFC championship game that season. The Eagles hadn't been to a championship since the 2008 season with Donovan McNabb. The Vikings hadn't made an appearance since 2009 with Brett Favre. As an additional incentive, Super Bowl LII was being held in Minneapolis, so the Vikings were trying to become the first team to play a Super Bowl in their home stadium.

Minnesota entered the game red hot, riding a four-game winning streak and coming off a victory for the ages in the divisional round. Early-round playoff games don't usually go down in NFL history, but that one will be talked about for a long time. It was an instant classic, dubbed the "Minnesota Miracle"—and rightly so.

With ten seconds left in their game against the visiting Saints, the Vikings trailed 24–23 at their own thirty-nine yard line. They had time for one last-gasp play. They needed lightning to strike, the planets to align—*anything*. History was not on their side. Since the NFL's inception in 1922, no team had ever scored a winning touchdown on the final play of the fourth quarter in the postseason.

Then Case Keenum, my good friend and former teammate, took the final snap of the game, dropped back in good protection, and hit receiver Stefon Diggs at the Saints' thirty-four yard line along the Vikings' sideline. The cornerback assigned to Diggs missed the attempted tackle and, in the process, took out the only other defender in the vicinity. Diggs pivoted, planted his hand on the ground to stay on his feet, and raced unchallenged to the end zone while 66,612 fans at U.S. Bank Stadium fell into utter delirium.

I watched the game on TV at home with Tori and my family, and when Diggs waltzed into the end zone, I just kept thinking, *Holy smokes*. No one could have predicted a play like that.

Believe it or not, watching that game was not a typical pastime for me. As a professional athlete who plays sports for a living, I need time away from sports whenever possible to maintain a healthy balance. But I watched that game for a few reasons—partly because it featured Case, who was a good friend, and Drew Brees, who also went to Westlake. Plus, we were scheduled to play the winner.

Once the game ended, I had to make a quick switch from spectator mode to preparation mode. The team that had just completely astonished me was now my opponent. And Minnesota was a formidable foe.

The Vikings had allowed only 3,078 passing yards in the regular season, second only to Jacksonville, and they'd allowed only thirteen touchdown passes—the best record in the league.

I knew right away that everyone was going to doubt us. We'd barely beaten Atlanta in a tough game of field position, and I hadn't thrown a touchdown pass since the first quarter of the Oakland game on Christmas Day—a whole month earlier.

Even after our win over the Falcons, the public negativity against me and our offense kicked right in:

"Foles can't throw the ball downfield!"

"If Foles doesn't take some deep shots, they're not going to beat Minnesota!"

"Philadelphia is just trying to cover up his weaknesses!"

"The Vikings are going to smack them!"

"The Vikings' defense is going to eat the Eagles whole!"

"Case Keenum, the guy who took over for Foles in St. Louis, is going to get the better of him again!"

"Minnesota is the best team in football. They're probably heading to the Super Bowl!"

On and on it went.

Admittedly, there was room for conjecture. I certainly hadn't played my best football since taking over for Carson. Plus, the Vikings had a highly skilled, aggressive defense, having led the league in scoring (15.8 points allowed per game), yards (275.9 allowed per game), and third-down percentage (25.2).

Even the NFL seemed to jump on the Vikings bandwagon. The week before the game, the league accidentally released a Super Bowl ad on social media that featured the images of Tom Brady and Case

Keenum, encouraging fans to give to one of its main charitable partners for a chance to "score two club-level seats to watch the Patriots
versus the Vikings battle it out for the coveted Super Bowl title!"

Talk about bulletin-board material. We put that up at our team
meeting and just let it sink in. Everyone was saying Philadelphia was
going to lose—even the NFL itself.

As I watched film, I was struck by their athleticism, their coverage skills, and their ability to communicate with each other and rally
to the ballcarrier. But I also knew what our offense was capable of.
As talented as their secondary players were, I was confident that our
receivers could beat them. Going in, our plan was to attack their
defense with everything we had and then keep at them until they
broke. That was Coach Pederson's mind-set, and it was mine, too.
We were going to come out of the gate fast, catch them off balance,
and then just keep pounding.

The game started off exactly how most people thought it would,
with Case leading Minnesota down the field on a perfect nine-play,
seventy-five-yard touchdown drive, capped off with a beautiful
twenty-five-yard pass to Kyle Rudolph in the end zone. At first blush,
it looked as though Minnesota was going to pick up where they left
off the week before.

We started a little slower on offense, punting the ball after a quick
possession. That's when our defense came through. On the Vikings'
next drive, Chris Long came around the outside corner and grazed
Case's right arm just as he was getting ready to throw. It wasn't a big
hit, but it disrupted his throwing motion just enough that he ended
up underthrowing the ball, and it was picked by Patrick Robinson,
who ran it back fifty yards for a touchdown. It was Patrick's fourth
interception of the year, and it couldn't have come at a better time.

The Vikings threatened again in the second, but once again, our defense came up big. Derek Barnett came around the outside and hit Case from behind, stripping the ball out of his hands in the red zone, and Chris Long recovered, ending the drive. From that point on, the momentum was ours. Minnesota never scored again, and we ran away with a 38–7 victory.

We completed more deep balls on them in one game (four passes of thirty yards or more) than they had allowed all season. It was just bombs away, up and down the field. I completed twenty-six of thirty-three passes for 352 yards and three touchdowns—including a fifty-three-yard score to Alshon Jeffery and a forty-one-yard flea-flicker to Torrey Smith—for a 141.4 passer rating. Overall, we racked up 456 yards of total offense, including twenty-seven first downs and ten of fourteen third-down conversions.

Honestly, those are the kinds of games you dream of playing. We exploded on offense, and everything came together perfectly. No one saw this coming—except us. We knew we had the ability to play at this level, and after three less-than-stellar offensive performances, we were finally able to make it happen. We just kept doing what we'd been doing all season: playing together as a team and never turning on each other. When you play that way, special things can happen.

The only downside to the game was a hit I took from Anthony Barr early in the third quarter, about three plays before I threw the flea-flicker to Torrey. It was a run-pass option play, and I should have handed it to the running back. Instead, I got a little greedy and threw the pass. My ribs paid the price, because Barr broke straight through the line and hammered me. The good news was that I was able to get the ball off in time, and I hit Alshon for a first down to keep the drive going. The bad news was that I was fairly certain I'd bruised my ribs. But when you're having a game like we were that day, the discomfort fades.

Immediately after the game, I sought out Case on the field. We'd become really close in St. Louis—as had Tori and Case's wife, Kimberly—and we'd kept in touch ever since. Since coming into the league as an undrafted free agent in 2012 following a phenomenal career at the University of Houston, Case had bounced around on various practice squads and active rosters and had changed teams four times in his first five seasons. That meant he understood the precarious nature of the NFL as much as I did. Add to that the fact that Case came into the year as a backup to Sam Bradford (who went down with an injury in week two), and we clearly had an awful lot in common.

When I finally caught up to him in the crowd, I gave him a huge hug and told him how proud I was of him.

"It couldn't have happened to a better person," he said with a huge smile on his face. "I'm really excited for you, Nick."

I'd been on the other side of that midfield embrace enough times to know how difficult it is, so Case's response spoke volumes to me about his character. He's a great player, but he's an even better person.

Meanwhile, back on the field, it was bedlam. Our fans were screaming, and confetti was raining down from above. I tried to take it all in. Game balls, trophies, and confetti definitely have their place, but seeing the joy on the fans' faces, celebrating with my team-mates, and watching my coaches hug their wives and kids and the players—those are the reasons you play the game.

Before the conference trophy presentation, I found Tori, and we had our own midfield celebration. All I could say was, "We did it!" Then the tears started to flow. We didn't say much more—there was no need to. Mostly we just held each other in disbelief, grateful that our journey had brought us to this point. For us, this was the culmination of so many emotions that had been building not just for months but for years—dealing with Tori's illness, getting traded to the Rams, being benched, almost quitting the game. Now Tori and I could finally take a deep breath and say, "Wow. This is unbelievable. Thank you, Jesus."

At the same time, I was also aware how quickly pride can take over. It's always there, lurking in the shadows, just waiting for an opportunity—a weak moment—to pounce. And that night I definitely felt a tug, a little voice inside nudging me toward arrogance: *See? I told you so. Why did you doubt your abilities? You've had it in you all along.*

But I quickly beat that pride down. For one thing, it wasn't true. Sure, we were going to the Super Bowl, but my contributions were no greater than anyone else's in the organization. Carson, Doug, Alshon, Frank, LeGarrette, Press, Jake, Jay, Nelson, Torrey, Zach, Fletcher, Kamu—every last guy on that roster and every coach, trainer, and assistant gave everything they had to get us to where we were, and no one could have done it alone.

By the time I got back to the locker room, the celebration was in full swing. Guys were hooting and hollering. Coach Pederson spoke to us briefly, and then, as we do after every game, we ended in the Lord's Prayer.

Then I checked in with the trainers. They took some X-rays, and I was right—it was bruised ribs. Considering what we got in return, I'd take it.

THE INVISIBLE MAN

I'm always famished after games—mostly because you have to eat so early on game days. I always stash a few nutrition bars in my locker just in case, but win or lose, as soon as that game clock expires, I have to eat.

Because it was late and we were both exhausted, I figured Tori and I would just go home and throw some chicken tenders in the oven, but my agent had booked a private room for us and the ten or so family members who were in town for the game. We were all going to meet at Del Frisco's downtown, just under four miles away from the stadium.

There was only one problem. How do you navigate Broad Street, the city's main artery, when nearly seventy thousand fans have just spilled out onto the street to celebrate the Eagles' first Super Bowl appearance in thirteen years, essentially turning South Philly into a northeastern Mardi Gras?

According to Philadelphia's finest, you don't.

"It's impossible," one officer said. "The street is shut down. There's no way you're going to get there."

His response sounded a little too much like the naysayers I'd been hearing since the Oakland game. Well, we didn't listen to the critics, and we'd just beaten the Vikings and their number one ranked defense by thirty-one points. Surely my friends and family could find a way to get to Del Frisco's for dinner.

Fortunately, my traveling party felt the same way. We found a side street off Interstate 95 and headed north, parking about a quarter of a mile away from the restaurant. It wasn't quite as crowded there as it was by the stadium, but there were still hordes of people and police everywhere.

Had I planned ahead a little more, I would have grabbed one of those rubber dog masks at the stadium to disappear into the crowd. Instead, I had to rely on my black beanie and eyeglasses for a disguise, while my six-foot-five brother-in-law, Ryan, walked closely in front of me. We probably passed by two dozen fans who were wearing my jersey, and nobody recognized me. By the next morning, my face would likely be plastered all over every newspaper in town, but for that night, I might as well have been the Invisible Man.

Once we got inside Del Frisco's, we had the place virtually to ourselves. We ate a lot of food, laughed, and had a great time reflecting on the game and the season. As much as I'd enjoyed celebrating with my teammates, it felt great just to relax, kick back, and hang out with loved ones.

Everything felt so surreal. I could hardly believe we'd just won the NFC championship. Was I really heading to Minneapolis in less than two weeks to face Tom Brady, Bill Belichick, and the Patriots (the greatest dynasty in NFL history) in the Super Bowl?

It didn't seem possible. Then again, the impossible had happened before. The question now was, could it happen one more time?

CHAPTER 12

THE WAITING GAME

Before Super Bowl LII, if you'd asked a hundred people who they thought would lead their team to victory—me or Tom Brady—I'll bet ninety-nine of them would have chosen Brady. The lone person to pick me? That would have been Tori. Well, our families would have picked me too. But you get the point.

On the surface, the pairing sounds like a total mismatch. One guy is the G.O.A.T.—a future first-ballot Hall of Famer with thirteen Pro Bowl invitations, three league MVPs, and five Super Bowl rings. The other guy? That would be me.

Don't get me wrong—I've had my share of successes as well. Still, statistically speaking, the deck was definitely stacked in the Patriots' favor. But just because a quarterback showdown looks obviously lop-sided on paper doesn't mean it will transpire that way. There are no guaranteed victories in the NFL. A lot can happen in sixty minutes, and that's why we play.

Besides, I knew going in that I had a stellar team around me.

FEELING PATRIOTIC

The AFC championship game between Jacksonville and New England was played before our conference title game on January 21. So when we beat Minnesota, we knew we'd be facing the Patriots in the Super Bowl.

Jacksonville had had a great season, and their defense played strong that year. In fact, up until the final few minutes, it looked like they were going to beat New England in the championship game. They were up 20–10 midway through the fourth quarter when Tom Brady did what he always seems to do—he led two late scoring drives and found Danny Amendola for touchdowns on both. That gave the Patriots a 24–20 win and the eighth Super Bowl appearance of the Belichick-Brady era. Like I said, there are no guaranteed victories in the NFL.

Personally, I was excited about playing the Patriots. Everyone wants to beat the best, and for the past decade, few teams have been better than New England. From the day Belichick and Brady both arrived in Foxborough back in 2000 through the 2017 season, the Patriots experienced only one losing season—their first, when they went 5–11 in 2000. In those seventeen years, they reached the play-offs fifteen times. Not only that, but they won 74 percent of their games, including a 26–10 record in the playoffs, and claimed five Lombardi Trophies. That's by far the greatest dynasty the sport has ever seen—even more decorated than Vince Lombardi's Packers, Don Shula's Dolphins, Chuck Noll's Steelers, Bill Walsh's 49ers, Joe Gibbs's Redskins, or Jimmy Johnson's Cowboys.

For the sake of perspective, when Bill and Tom won their first Super Bowl together on February 3, 2002—a 20–17 victory over Kurt Warner and the St. Louis Rams, thanks to Adam Vinatieri's memorable forty-eight-yard field goal as time expired—I was still in middle school, having just turned thirteen. In other words, these guys have been doing this for a long time.

Would it have been easier to face off against a rookie quarterback who had limited playing experience and a little less bling on his fingers? Sure. But where was the fun in that? I wanted to go against the best in the world. I wanted the opportunity to measure ourselves against the gold standard of our sport.

Naturally, the general consensus leading into the game was, "Might as well give the Patriots their rings now." But in spite of all the criticism and doubt outside our locker room in the two weeks before the game, we were going into it focused, confident, and ready to win.

It was going to be David against Goliath.

And we all know how that one turned out.

ELIMINATE THE NEGATIVE

I'm sure it's hard for fans to wait two weeks between the conference championships and the Super Bowl. But for players, the extra week is critical. After four preseason games, sixteen regular-season games, and two postseason games, virtually everyone on our roster was a little banged up, so that week gave us a little time to rest and recover. I was especially grateful for the time to let my sore ribs heal.

Besides the physical toll, championship games require a lot of emotional energy. In terms of mental preparation alone, those extra seven days are vital. Because once you get to the actual Super Bowl site, it's pure chaos.

NFL athletes are notorious for being creatures of habit. We need a method to our madness. So during the first week of Super Bowl preparation (in which teams stay in their home cities), we kept our normal rhythms, as if we were playing a Monday night game. So after a two-day break, we resumed activities on Wednesday, doing what we would typically do on a Tuesday. Thursday's activities were what we'd do on a Wednesday, and so on. Aside from being offset by one day, everything else was business as usual—team meetings, film study, fundamental drills, and practice.

What was *not* normal was the media presence. That entire week, reporters were documenting our every move. We were lucky if we had ten minutes to ourselves at our lockers after practice before the media swarm descended on us for about an hour. Most of the questions were about whether we could keep building on what we did against Minnesota and why we'd played so well in the playoffs up to this point. And then there were all the questions about how I almost retired from the game. But this was just the appetizer: the full media smorgasbord was awaiting us in Minneapolis, the site of the Super Bowl. That's why our goal was to get the physical and mental heavy lifting done at home and leave the fine-tuning for the following week. I was grateful for people within the organization who had ridden this rodeo before—Chris Maragos had been to a Super Bowl with Seattle, Malcom Jenkins had made an appearance with New Orleans, and Doug had played in a few himself. Thanks to them, we knew that once we were on site, the distractions would multiply exponentially.

For my part, I wanted to do everything I could to block out unnecessary distractions. During the two weeks leading up to the Super Bowl, I didn't answer any texts or emails, and I didn't read any stories related to the game. I was 100 percent focused. The only news I got came from the questions reporters asked me.

Tori did a great job handling all the tickets, hotels, and flights for friends and family members who were coming to the game, and believe me, that was an enormous undertaking. There was also the task of figuring out who we could bring to the game in the first place since we only had a certain number of tickets allotted to us. She handled these logistics seemingly around the clock for the week before the game, and it was pretty chaotic. I don't know how the single guys handled it.

I also faced another distraction: sponsorship requests. Suddenly the offers started flooding in—anything from wearing a certain brand of headphones during pregame warmups to playing a video game with fans on site at the Super Bowl. In the time since the clock had expired in the championship game, around twenty companies had contacted my agent with offers.

Though the financial opportunities were tempting, I was hesitant, in part because of the lessons I'd learned during my Pro Bowl season in 2013. It was awesome to be able to represent companies I admired, but I knew from experience how much time and focus that required. There would be plenty of time for that in the off-season. This was the time to get ready for the biggest game of my life.

One evening when Tori and I were on our way home from our date night, my marketing agent called with six pages of marketing opportunities to go over. Throughout the conversation, I was praying for God's direction. He was about halfway through his list of offers when I interrupted him.

"Hold on," I said. "Let's stop right there."

"What's up?" he asked.

"I know these are great opportunities, but I'm going to say no to every single one of them."

He was shocked.

I couldn't blame him. It was easy money—and a lot of it. But in my mind, accepting even one of them would have subconciously taken my energy away from the game. For one thing, a lot of the agreements wouldn't go into effect until after the Super Bowl was over. I'd still get paid if we lost, but I'd get paid more if we won. I didn't want that to affect me at all—not even a fraction of a percent. I wanted every ounce of my focus to be on preparing for the Super Bowl. I didn't care about the money; all I cared about was being the best player and teammate I could be in the biggest game of my life.

"Don't you want me to go through the rest of the list?" he asked. He was doing his job—and he was doing it well. But I'd made up my mind.

"No, I don't," I replied. "Because quite frankly, I don't care what the dollar amount is. I'm going into this game to win. The Patriots are really good, and I need to go right at them with everything I've got."

I didn't want to look back after it was all over and think, *I said yes to something so silly that affected my preparation.*

Right before I left for Minneapolis, Tori and I went on our weekly date night—this time to Zahav, a modern Israeli restaurant in Philadelphia—and we took Lily with us. This restaurant is tough to get into, but we managed to get a quiet table in the corner, where we enjoyed a nice, low-key dinner.

As we were getting ready to leave, Tori and I noticed the servers congregating near the front. Suddenly, everyone in the restaurant stood up, turned toward us, and started to applaud. It was a Super Bowl send-off. Nobody had come up to our table the entire time we were there—not a single autograph seeker, well-wisher, or fan hoping for a quick selfie. And then, *boom*—we had this really cool show of support as we were leaving. It was almost like a mini pep rally from my high school days—a nice moment with fans who wanted us to know they were behind us all the way.

Once we were outside, I looked at Tori. "I don't know if anything's ever going to be the same again, sweetheart."

She nodded and smiled. "I know."

COMING IN COLD

Super Bowl week was unlike anything I'd ever experienced. How do you put into words what every young football player dreams about from the first time he picks up a ball?

I guess you look for the mundane—like walking onto the airplane.

Only there's nothing mundane about the Super Bowl. Everything is big and flashy and ostentatious. In fact, even the plane ride was far from ordinary.

We touched down in Minneapolis on Sunday afternoon. Normally we disembark outside and then leave the airport by bus. In this case, though, we were brought into a large hangar where a bunch of reporters were gathered behind ropes to film us walking off the plane. That's when it really began to sink in: *Wow, I'm heading to the Super Bowl!*

Ron Jaworski was there to welcome us, and a representative from the NFL was at the bottom of the stairs handing each of us a cold-weather hat with the Super Bowl LII logo on it. We needed it, too. Normally the Super Bowl takes place in a warm climate, like Florida, California, Texas, or Louisiana. In fact, only six of the fifty-two Super Bowls have been held in northern cities—two in Detroit, one in Indianapolis, one in New Jersey, and now two in Minneapolis.

All week long, the temperature hovered right around zero degrees, and with the wind chill, the "real feel" temperature was around nega-tive twenty. Granted, we would be playing inside, but it was still going to be rather brisk walking to and from the venues. Just making the fifty-yard trek from the hangar to the bus chilled my blood. Why the media felt the need to film a bunch of football players in street clothes and heavy coats walking from a hangar to a bus in subzero weather, I'll never know. Then again, it *was* the Super Bowl, so all bets were off.

Case in point: when we reached our hotel, the Radisson Blu at the Mall of America, there was actually a military tank parked outside, and the place was crawling with soldiers and Secret Service. I'm sure it should have made us all feel safe, but there was something discon-certing about seeing that much security in one place.

It was also a little unnerving to walk into the lobby and see a giant picture of my teammates and me hanging behind the check-in counter. My teammates and I are all pretty low-key guys, so this was going to take some getting used to. For the most part we were able to laugh it off and think, *Wow, what is happening here?*

Once I got situated in my room, I needed to attend to a very important matter: coffee. Before leaving for Minneapolis, I had con-tacted Bulletproof, and they'd sent two massive care packages with everything I'd need to make my coffee. Like I said, football players are creatures of habit, and there was no way I was going to alter my morning ritual during the biggest week of my life. Besides, if there was ever a week I needed to be Bulletproofed, this was it.

After dinner, Carson, Nate, Frank, Press, Spencer, and I all needed an escape, so aptly enough, we found an escape room at the Mall of America. If you've never experienced this phenomenon before, it's kind of like a live-action mystery. Basically, you're locked in a room and you have sixty minutes to find and decipher clues in order to get out. Carson has done at least twenty of these, and he's a pro. I, on the other hand, was clearly a rookie.

After spending so much time together locked away in that little quarterback sanctuary, you might think we'd want to get away from each other for a while, but I honestly can't think of another group of guys I'd rather be locked in a room with. Besides, with everything else that was going on, it was fun to do something completely unrelated to football for a change.

Come Monday morning, though, it was back to business as usual. Each day started at 5 a.m. I'd wake up and start a pot of coffee in our makeshift quarterbacks meeting room at the hotel, and then at 5:45 or 6, I'd start watching film—mostly of the Patriots' defense. After a few hours of film work, I'd head to our team meeting at 8:45. From there, it was a full day of practice, lifting, and walk-throughs at the University of Minnesota, followed by more meetings and film study. Each day was packed until about 6 or 6:30 p.m. Outside of training camp, it was probably the most intense week of football I'd ever experienced.

After dinner, I'd come back to my hotel room and hop in the tub for a thirty-minute Epsom salt bath to let my body recover. Most nights I'd also spend time reading a devotional or talking to Tori on the phone. Afterward, I'd read a little more in bed, pray, and be asleep by 9 or 9:15 p.m. It was more essential than ever that I get some rest. When you're preparing for a game of this magnitude, the extra pressure alone can make it feel like you're carrying a three-hundred-pound gorilla on your back all day.

Off the field, Super Bowl festivities officially kicked off on Monday with Opening Night at the Xcel Energy Center in St. Paul, where the NHL's Minnesota Wild plays. This is the event formerly known as media day, where hundreds, if not thousands, of media outlets from around the world descend to unearth and dissect every possible storyline from both teams. It's an incredible spectacle, and a lot of wacky stuff can happen. Believe it or not, I actually saw one guy interviewing players while wearing a shark costume.

When our team first got introduced onstage, there were a lot of boos and "Skol" chants from the crowd—a dead giveaway that lots of Vikings fans were out there. Then the Patriots joined us onstage, and Brady, Belichick, and I all shook hands for a photo opp.

I'd only faced off against the Patriots a couple of times in my career, and those were preseason games that Brady only played a series or two in, so standing up there onstage with the two of them was a little surreal. Even so, I wasn't intimidated. Yeah, they were good—maybe even the best—but on any given Sunday, I knew my teammates and I could do just as much damage as they could. We were clearly the underdogs in this matchup, but we were the most confident group of underdogs ever assembled.

Once the media started asking questions, things got pretty crazy. First they had Tom and me sit next to each other on the stage, along with my teammate Malcolm Jenkins and New England's Devin McCourty as moderators from the NFL Network and ESPN asked questions. The first thing they asked Tom was what advice he would give me heading into my first Super Bowl. Tom replied, "He knows what to do. He's a professional quarterback. He's a great player. Obviously his team has a ton of confidence in him. He's had a great playoff season. He's been a great player since he came into the league. . . . I know he'll do a great job."

I'd been a fan of Tom's since I was a kid—and I told him that onstage—so to hear him say that in front of thousands of people meant a lot to me. Of course, being a Michigan grad, he also got in a quick dig at Michigan State, but it was all in fun—he couldn't have been more gracious.

After that, I went to a different area to do an individual Q and A session with reporters. That was a total free-for-all. The questions ranged from serious to downright absurd. One woman from *Extra* asked me to reach into a helmet of questions and pick one. At first I declined, but when she persisted, I obliged. The question: Could I name any of the characters on *Game of Thrones*? (For the record, I've never seen it.) Another reporter asked me who my favorite Teenage Mutant Ninja Turtle was. I used to love watching that show as a kid, but the question caught me so off guard, I drew a complete blank. (In case you're wondering, it was Michelangelo.)

At one point, a guy sidled up on my right and asked if I'd read Tom's book, *The TB12 Method*. Conveniently, he had a copy and set it on the podium for me. Then he asked when I was going to publish my own cookbook. I had to break it to him that it hadn't really crossed my mind. Then he asked me to sign Tom's book. Given that Tom himself was somewhere nearby—probably telling someone from Nickelodeon who his favorite Power Ranger was—it seemed like a strange request. I didn't feel comfortable signing the front cover, so I signed the back. All night long, weird stuff like that kept happening.

At one point, though, I had a genuine opportunity to share my faith. Someone in the media throng must have read my YouVersion devotional about 2 Corinthians 12:9 ("'My grace is all you need. My power works best in weakness.' So now I am glad to boast about my weaknesses, so that the power of Christ can work through me"). Up to that point, I hadn't talked much in public about stepping away from the game. Now that this reporter was asking me about it, I had a chance to expound on my faith journey. It probably seemed strange for me to be talking about embracing weakness there, of all places. Which might explain what happened next.

Once the story went public, the media ran with that angle for the rest of the week. It was as though someone had stood up and shouted, "Stop the presses! Quarterback who briefly left football is now playing in the Super Bowl!" The next thing I knew, every reporter who approached me wanted to talk about my faith—and believe me, that was far more humbling and exciting than anything else that happened that week. I never expected the interviews to go that route, but I couldn't have been more thrilled.

For the next three days, I did daily fifteen- to twenty-minute press conferences. I expected the Super Bowl experience to be intense, but I hadn't anticipated such a barrage of off-the-field responsibilities. As happy as I was to see Tori and Lily when they arrived, I only got to see them briefly. About twenty-five people—our family and close friends—came into town to support me that weekend, but my schedule was so packed that I didn't get to see anyone except my immediate family. Still, it was nice to know I had so many people in town, cheering me on.

PLAY CALLS FROM AN ANCIENT BOOK

It wasn't just the media frenzy around me that had me amped up; there was also a lot going on internally. As the clock started ticking down toward kickoff, I felt a bit trapped in my own emotions. I'd never experienced something on the scale of the Super Bowl before, and I wasn't sure how to sort through it all.

During the first week of preparations while I was still in Philadelphia, I talked to Tori about how I was doing. When I was feeling down or stressed, she would remind me that God had brought us to this point for a reason and that he was using our story to impact people. "Stay the course," she told me. "Take it day by day, just like you've been doing." She was right—no one could have made up what we'd lived thus far, and God's hand was apparent in every detail. We needed to keep trusting and let God write the rest of the story.

I also talked to my brothers-in-law, since they understood the athletics side of things and I knew they believed in me. Then there were the phone calls with my dad. He has always been an inspiration to me and a role model for what you can achieve if you work hard and put your mind to it. But as grateful as I was for all the people supporting me, even they weren't enough of an outlet for my emotions.

I found what I needed in the Psalms. If you're not familiar with the Bible, the Psalms are a collection of 150 songs, many of which were written by King David (of David and Goliath fame). I've always felt a visceral connection with King David, mostly because I see a lot of parallels between David's life journey and my own. I'm not saying I'm royalty or anything, but the feelings resonate. God took David from a place of complete anonymity as a shepherd and graciously raised him to a place of great distinction as a king. Along the way, David experienced moments of great joy as well as terrible suffering, which he wrote about in his psalms. I saw a lot of David's heart reflected in my own journal entries, and his wisdom, faith, and sincerity have always been an encouragement to me.

Rereading the Psalms brought me a sense of peace and perspective in those days leading up to the Super Bowl. In David, I saw a man who had endured far more than I had. He was constantly in danger, yet he continued to place his trust in God. He was a great soldier and a skillful leader. He unified a nation and lifted it to great heights. Yet he was utterly human. He committed terrible sins, and he struggled with constant doubts and fears. But when placed in difficult circumstances, he showed extreme faith in God, and that gave him the courage and the strength to go on.

My challenge was not against giants or jealous kings, but in my own way, I needed extreme faith too.

Leading up to the game, one of the films I studied was Super Bowl LI—New England's remarkable 34–28 overtime victory against Atlanta. The Falcons led 28–3 midway through the third quarter. At that point, everyone thought the game was over. But the Patriots just kept chipping away. What struck me about that game was that no lead is safe against a team like New England. You can never hit the brakes, play it safe, or run out the clock. You have to play aggressively the entire game, as if the score is always tied 0–0. That's not easy to do. As history has shown, most of New England's opponents haven't been able to.

As I prepared to face the greatest dynasty the sport had ever seen, I wasn't consumed with worry or doubt. But I knew the stage would be very big and very bright, and winning would require every ounce of effort we could give. Nothing less would suffice.

I also knew I needed lots of prayer. With David's psalms as my model, I frequently went to God in prayer that week. But I never asked for victory—that would have been presumptuous and self-serving. Instead, my constant request was, "God, help me to glorify you in everything I do. Please drive out all my fear. Help me play with boldness. Whether we win or lose, I want you to get all the praise. And if we win, please keep me humble and help me stay focused on you."

Yes, I wanted to win—badly. I would do everything possible to help my team reach that goal. And I certainly felt the weight of the moment. The expectations of a franchise, a city, and millions of passionate fans were riding on the shoulders of my teammates and me.

But regardless of Sunday's outcome, I knew that I would be content. I knew that God had a plan for me that exceeded anything that could happen on a football field. It took a while for me to understand that, but once I did, it was incredibly freeing.

Sunday was fast approaching. But strengthened by the words of David, I felt ready—almost uncannily ready—and peaceful. This wasn't a contentment I could generate on my own. This was God's peace.

I was ready to play. After two weeks of media obligations, practices, and mental preparation, it was go time. No more training. No more interviews. No more analyzing. It was time to get out on the field.

Win or lose, I was in a good place.

CHAPTER 13

FEELING SUPER

8:45 a.m.

This is usually late morning for me. Most days during the season, I wake up early enough to rouse a rooster. But on the morning of February 4, 2018—Super Bowl Sunday—I told the rooster to put a sock in it. My body needed as much rest as possible for the task ahead. So I slept in until almost 9 a.m.

Kickoff was set for 6:30 p.m., so my goal was to try to remain calm for the long day ahead. Breakfast was my beloved coffee and a four-egg omelet with cheese, bacon, and spinach. I spent most of the morning in my room reading the Bible, praying, journaling, playing music, and listening to a YouVersion devotional called "Making Sense of God" by Timothy Keller, a pastor in New York. I also reviewed our team game plan.

I tried not to think too much—I wanted to stay in the moment and not get distracted. I meditated on Matthew 6:34: "Don't worry about tomorrow, for tomorrow will bring its own worries. Today's trouble is enough for today." As I've learned throughout my career, worry produces nothing beneficial. If anything, it reveals a lack of trust in God. As the biggest moment of my career approached, my goal was to get all the negative thoughts out of my mind so I could play with a clear head—for God's glory.

When I finally walked onto the U.S. Bank Stadium field two hours before kickoff, the scene was stunning. You couldn't miss the huge banners of Tom Brady and me hanging from the rafters. It kind of reminded me of that scene in *Rocky* when Rocky walks into the Philadelphia Spectrum the night before the fight and sees two giant posters—one of himself and one of Apollo Creed—hanging up over the ring. I've probably seen that movie half a dozen times, but I never understood how Rocky felt at that moment until now. It was pretty unbelievable.

That wasn't the only departure from a normal game-day experience. Hundreds of fans were already starting to pour into the stands, and the field was swarming with media. A nearby Darius Rucker concert was broadcasting live on the stadium Jumbotrons, which was fun for me—I've been a big fan ever since he was the lead singer of Hootie and the Blowfish.

No one from the media spoke directly to me, but one reporter did grab Nate Sudfeld and pull him off to the side. The two chatted for about ten minutes before the guy mentioned something about Nate being at the 2012 Senior Bowl with Kirk Cousins and Russell Wilson. Only Nate wasn't at the 2012 Senior Bowl—I was.

"Uh, you do know I'm not Nick, right?" Nate said politely.

Poor guy.

The funniest part is that the same reporter had interviewed Nate six days earlier during the Opening Night festivities. People say we look so much alike we could pass as brothers, which meant Nate had to deal with more than his share of mix-ups toward the end of the season.

Despite the distractions around me, I tried to block everything out and focus on my regular pregame routine with Spencer Phillips, Coach Pederson's assistant. We have a tradition of tossing the football back and forth to get warmed up—kind of like kids playing backyard football together. It's a simple routine, but it helps me get my mind and body right. Meanwhile, I was jamming to Darius Rucker tunes. I was in my element, and my adrenaline was pumping.

Later, as Pink sang *The Star-Spangled Banner*, I tried to absorb all the scenery and pageantry: the stadium packed with nearly seventy thousand fans, the huge American flag displayed over the field, the military flyover, and the Patriots standing on the other sideline.

Even though they were technically the home team, New England had opted to wear their white road jerseys. Rumor had it they'd never lost a Super Bowl while wearing white before. Since we had yet to lose a postseason game while wearing our midnight green home jerseys, their decision was fine by us. Whatever happened, the streak would end for someone that night.

Well, I thought as I soaked in the surroundings, *this is as big as it gets.* I didn't feel overwhelmed, just impressed.

A few lingering questions bubbled to the surface, though. How was I going to react during the game? How would my mind and body respond under pressure? Would I be able to channel all this adrenaline into something positive?

There's no way to really know. I was hopeful, and I tried to remain confident. But as a first-time Super Bowl participant, I had no idea how I'd react to the pressure and emotions once the game started.

The year before, I watched Super Bowl LI between New England

and Atlanta on TV. I was still a backup with the Chiefs then, and I figured I'd be staying in Kansas City for the 2017 season. And now here I was in Super Bowl LII playing with the Eagles again and starting against Tom Brady and the Patriots. Talk about an amazing turn of events.

GETTING IN THE ZONE

The Patriots—who entered the game as 5.5-point favorites—won the pregame coin toss and deferred the opening kickoff to us. Our first offensive play was a three-man route called "*y* motion to trips right pepper all lightning." It's the same play we used to convert a crucial third-and-eight pass before running out the clock against the Rams in week fourteen. The play was designed to get Alshon Jeffery an early reception for ten yards to kick-start our momentum. But the Patriots' defensive back had some help over the top, so Alshon was covered. I quickly reset my feet and hit Nelson Agholor for a four-yard completion.

Four yards . . . big deal, right? Well, it *was* a big deal because it showed me how quickly my body was reacting and that I was ready to roll. It was a great confidence boost.

My focus throughout the game would be to play as aggressively as possible and to not worry about the clock. I would allow myself an occasional peek, but I wasn't going to be glued to it. I was going to keep pushing hard until it said 0:00 in the fourth quarter. Given Brady's reputation for fourth-quarter comebacks and what had happened against Atlanta last year, I knew we needed to score as many points as possible.

We ran fourteen plays on our opening drive—mostly short passes and runs by Jay Ajayi—and managed to keep the Patriots' offense off the field for more than seven minutes. Unfortunately, our drive stalled on the New England seven, and we had to settle for a field goal. Don't get me wrong—it's always great to get points on the board, especially on your opening drive, but in the back of my mind, I knew field goals weren't going to cut it. In all likelihood, this game would not be a low-scoring affair. If we wanted to win this thing, we were going to have to take some shots.

On our next possession, that's exactly what we did. After LeGarrette Blount put us into great field position with a thirty-six-yard run to the New England thirty-four, I swung for the fences.

The play call was pretty simple. It was a play-action pass from a single-back formation with Alshon split out wide left in what we call a slot formation. At the snap, Alshon would run an outside release post route against man coverage to the end zone, although the play wasn't designed to go automatically to Alshon. If I had played it by the book, I probably would have hit a deep crossing route coming from the other direction. But my instincts and trust in my teammate told me otherwise. I figured Alshon, who was in one-on-one coverage, would win a jump ball in the end zone, so I launched one thirty-four yards downfield. Sure enough, Alshon made a spectacular grab at the back of the end zone.

That's what playing this game at the highest level is all about—reacting to your gut, taking some chances, and letting your receivers, who are the best in the world, do their thing.

After our missed extra point and a subsequent missed field goal attempt by the Patriots, we went into the second quarter ahead 9–3.

LeGarrette rumbled twenty-one yards for a touchdown in our second series of the second quarter, but thanks to my lone interception of the playoffs, New England scored on back-to-back possessions to make it 15–12 with just over two minutes left before halftime.

Momentum seemed to be swinging New England's way, and giving Tom Brady and Bill Belichick momentum can be deadly. We needed to take control again.

We needed to try something special.

AN INSTANT CLASSIC

I have a hunch Eagles fans will be talking about the Philly Special decades from now. But that play might not have materialized without the talents of an undrafted rookie who, frankly, had the game of his life that night.

It was the third play of our drive, and I threw a touch pass to Corey Clement on a rail route right up the sideline. He proceeded to break two tackles, including one vicious stiff-arm, and turned what could have been a simple eight- or ten-yard gain into a beautiful fifty-five-yard catch-and-run inside the Patriots' ten. We tried three times to punch the ball into the end zone—twice on the ground, and once through the air—but without success.

Facing fourth and goal from the one yard line with thirty-eight seconds left before the half, we called a time-out. The safe call would have been to attempt a field goal and take a six-point lead. In fact, that's what most of the broadcasters were calling for us to do. But all season, Doug Pederson had shown tremendous faith in our offense. He wasn't afraid to take a risk every once in a while, and he definitely wasn't about to play it safe now.

I walked up to him and said, "You want to try the Philly Special?" Basically, it was a trick play where I would line up in the shotgun, but instead of the snap going to me, the ball would go to Corey, and he would flip it to tight end Trey Burton, who would then throw it to me.

We installed the play during our playoff bye week, and the first time we ran it was during a walk-through. When we executed the play during the practice, the mechanics weren't quite right—how I did the check, the cadence, and other little nuances. We needed to fine-tune a lot of details in order to fool the defense.

After that first attempt, the coaches told me, "You need to give us a little more acting next time."

I'll admit, my performance wasn't exactly worthy of an Oscar, but hey, we're football guys, not Hollywood types. Anyway, each time I did the play, I improved my theatrics, making my pre-snap role seem more believable. And that was the key. If I drew too much attention to myself, the defense would know something was up.

Fine-tuning the play took a few weeks, and we only ran it two or three times full speed in practice. Then we ran it a few more times in walk-throughs. That might not sound like a lot of rehearsals, but that's normal when a team has so many plays to nail down during game planning.

I had the play in the back of my mind going into the game, and I was pumped to use it. But it had to be the right time. Originally, we viewed it as more of a second-half call—something we could try when we wanted to go up by two scores, probably on a second- or third-and-short situation. But when New England started creeping up on us near halftime, the time seemed right.

I should mention that the play didn't originate with us. It has been used under different names and in slightly different formations both at the college level and in the NFL for years. Even the Patriots tried a version of the play a few series earlier, but Danny Amendola's pass ended up floating just beyond Brady's fingertips. The point is, a lot of other teams have tried it. We were just the ones who made it legendary.

Coach Pederson mulled it over for a few seconds. This was a big moment. If we were to score a touchdown now, it would be a huge boost. But if we walked away with nothing, it could be a decision we'd regret for years to come.

Finally, after what felt like an eternity, Coach Pederson nodded and said, "Yeah. Let's do it."

I ran out to the huddle, leaned in, and said, "All right, here we go. Philly Special. Ready?"

They all nodded. "Ready!"

We broke, knowing this was it.

As soon as the whistle blew, we lined up in shotgun formation. Corey lined up next to me, and then I shifted him to right behind. Trey was split out several yards past the left side of our offensive line and a couple of steps behind wide receiver Torrey Smith, at the line of scrimmage. Alshon was split out to the right side of the formation on the ball.

Before the snap, as I called out several cadences, I walked up to the right side of the offensive line behind tackle Lane Johnson. Quarterbacks sometimes walk up to the line to give specific directions to linemen or to call audible plays before heading back behind the center for the snap, so as far as the Patriots were concerned, everything was normal. And herein lies the beauty—and the deception—of the Philly Special: I never went back behind the center to receive the snap.

Instead, as I walked to the line, I called out several cadences: "Easy, easy . . . kill, kill . . . Lane, Lane!" Some signals were real; some were decoys. The second call of *Lane* was the code word for center Jason Kelce to snap the ball. By the time I shouted *Lane* twice, I had set myself behind the call's namesake. This was our way for me to issue the snap call, because we didn't want a running back to do it and show our hand.

The play worked to perfection. Jason snapped the ball to Corey, who pulled the defense left by running that way while Trey swept right to receive the pitch from Corey. While the play was developing, I waited motionless for a second at the line of scrimmage before running a drag route into the end zone. Meanwhile, Alshon ran into the end zone and to the left, drawing the only defender on that side of the field away from me. That's when Trey, rolling to his right, found me with a beautifully thrown pass just as I crossed the goal line.

The whole offensive unit executed the play flawlessly, but what made the play especially meaningful for me was the fact that Trey was the one who threw me the ball.

Trey's nickname on the team is Treybow. A dual-threat quarterback coming out of high school, he went to the University of Florida and was going to be the next Tim Tebow. But thanks to his versatility, he was moved to a variety of different positions.

Trey arrived in Philadelphia as an undrafted free agent in 2014, the third and final year of my first stint with the Eagles, and he mostly played on special teams. I saw him at Zach Ertz's wedding in March 2017, less than two weeks after I had re-signed with the Eagles, and he shared with me what an impact it had on him to see the starting quarterback leading the Bible study in 2014. That meant a lot to me.

When I rejoined the group later that year, I was excited to see that Trey had taken a larger role in the Bible study and that he and his wife, Yesenia, were working with International Justice Mission fighting sex trafficking worldwide. Trey is an amazing guy, and getting to share that moment with him made an already incredible play feel that much more special.

Interestingly, we talked about using the Philly Special long before the Super Bowl. It was an option on our call sheet for the NFC championship in the event that we needed to increase our lead in the second half. But because we already had a big lead against Minnesota, we decided to save it. It was also on the call sheet against Atlanta the prior week, but it was still a newer play that needed refinement, so we weren't quite ready to use it yet.

Teams often put trick plays on the call sheet several weeks before using them, just as a reminder that they're available. Ultimately, though, plays like that are best used infrequently and at very specific times—otherwise, you lose the element of surprise.

The odds that the Patriots' offense and ours would both try similar plays in one game are probably a million to one. Of course, the fact that they tried it first and were unsuccessful probably made our attempt that much more of a surprise.

One thing's for sure: the Philly Special definitely caught the Patriots off guard. After the game, I watched the video of the play with the sound turned on, and you could hear them saying, "Man, that was a good play call" and "Oh wow, they got us on that one."

After the play, I brought the ball we used for the Philly Special to the sidelines and gave it to our equipment guy because I wanted Trey's kids to have a keepsake. Now I think the NFL is putting it in the Hall of Fame, but hey, that's not a bad problem to have.

Thanks to the Philly Special, we went into halftime leading 22–12. There was still a lot of football left to play, but we were feeling great.

BACK AND FORTH

Fans might love the Super Bowl halftime show, but for players it's a long wait—thirty minutes or so, about double the length of a normal halftime. Our coaches met together for about half that time, and then they came out and talked to us. Coach Pederson informed us about a few second-half adjustments, but mostly he kept the message really simple: keep attacking, continue to play for each other, stay confident, and they can't stop us. After that, we just focused on hydrating and waited for the second half to start.

The Patriots got the ball first, and less than three minutes into the third quarter, Brady found tight end Rob Gronkowski for a five-yard score to cut our lead to 22–19. Clearly, the Patriots weren't just going to roll over.

Then again, neither were we.

We responded with a nice mixture of runs from LeGarrette and Jay, along with some key completions, to move the ball well into New England territory. Then, on third and six from the twenty-two, we decided to take a shot in the end zone.

We split Corey out to the left side to see who was going to cover him, and then we returned him to the backfield pre-snap to recognize the coverage. It was man coverage—what the play was designed for—so this was perfect. We wanted the linebacker to think this was a normal running back check, and then we'd have Corey give him a good stutter move and run right past him for a touchdown.

When I dropped back, I held the safety for a count and then shifted my vision to Corey on his route. I saw Corey was triple-covered, and I thought, *Oh wow, this looks horrible. This isn't what we thought it would look like in man coverage.* Then the safety briefly hesitated, and I thought, *Wait, I can fit it in there—I'm gonna rip it.*

Of course, all of this happened in a fraction of a second. But that's exactly what I did. The ball went right past two defenders, with another in the near vicinity, and Corey made a great catch while falling into the end zone. It was just one more reminder to me to listen to my instincts and react accordingly. When my brain says, *Fire it!* I just need to let it fly. No thinking about it. No second-guessing. Just fire.

Of course, if you were looking at that play on paper, there's no way I should have thrown it to Corey. But because I was reacting more than thinking, *boom*—touchdown. We were now up 29–19.

We continued trading blows with the Patriots—another touchdown pass by Brady, followed by a field goal by Jake to put us up six again. But when Brady hit Gronk for a four-yard score with 9:22 left in the game, New England took its first lead of the game, 33–32.

This surprised no one. After all, they're the Patriots. That's what they do. You can never count them out. At that point, all of America—particularly those in Atlanta—were probably thinking, *Here they go again.*

But our offense was about to take the field, and as I waited on the sideline, all I was thinking was, *Here* we *go again.* I wasn't worried about the score. I wasn't worried about the time. I knew we were about to get the ball back, and we were going to keep charging. *If anyone in America thinks this game is over,* I thought, *then they don't know us very well.*

ZACH ATTACK

The kinds of plays that are typically immortalized are touchdowns and turnovers. But in our game-winning drive, there were several plays that didn't result in points but were every bit as critical as those that did.

The first was a fourth-and-one situation from our own forty-five yard line with 5:39 remaining. Coach Pederson called one of my favorite plays, a crossing concept, and I was able to get through my progression, move around a little bit, and buy Zach enough time to make a play.

Here's the thing: if you put the ball anywhere in Zach's zip code, he's going to haul it in and do something with it. And that's exactly what he did. We needed one yard; he got two. That was a crucial first down. If the Patriots had gotten the ball there, it could have been game over. They already owned a one-point lead, and Brady is a master at milking the clock. But once again, Coach Pederson showed a lot of trust in us, and we made it work.

Another key non-scoring play during that drive came three plays later, when I hit Nelson on a second-window slant route right up the middle for a big gain. We were thinking it would be man coverage, but they went zone. Even though our play wasn't the best fit for the coverage, it felt like Nelly and I were just playing ball in a back lot together, and he made a great catch. He gained eighteen yards and brought us inside field goal range to the twenty-four yard line with less than three minutes to play.

At that point, I started experiencing some inner conflict. Part of me was thinking, *Look at the clock. We've got it. Let's just finish this thing.* But I had to remind myself, *No, we have to keep going. Don't believe this game is over. We need to score another touchdown. Stay in the moment, and execute the next play.*

After three more plays, we were facing third and seven at the eleven yard line. A field goal would give us a two-point lead, but there would still be more than two minutes remaining. And that's an eternity for someone like Brady. So Doug dialed up another great play. It didn't hurt that it was going to a guy with two of the surest hands in football.

Zach had been making big plays for us all season. He was a rookie during my Pro Bowl season in 2013 and immediately made an impact. You could tell even back then that he was going to be a great player, and now he was about to prove what he was made of.

The play Doug ordered was a combination of a quick screen on one side and Zach on a slant route to the left, with the running back in motion pre-snap to the right. There was a lot going on for a quick-completion play. We had three receivers in a bunch formation on the right and then sent Corey in motion to the same side. That left Zach, who was split out wide left, isolated in one-on-one man coverage. And Zach Ertz vs. *anybody* for eleven yards on a slant route isn't even a contest. I'll take that bet any day of the week, and twice on Super Bowl Sunday.

In typical Ertzian fashion, Zach beat his defensive back, caught the ball around the seven yard line, took several steps, and dove with outstretched arms into the end zone, just as the defender, who had stumbled to the turf, desperately lunged at his legs. Once Zach broke the plane of the goal line and hit the ground, the ball popped into the air. Zach rolled onto his back and caught it, never allowing it to touch the ground. We all started celebrating, but our joy turned to trepidation as we saw the referee heading to the sideline review booth.

I'm not going to lie. There was a split second when I couldn't help but think, *You've got to be kidding me. There's no way that's not a touchdown. If this isn't a touchdown, then I don't understand this game.*

Of course, it's happened before. Perhaps the most famous was Dez Bryant's non-catch in the 2014 NFC divisional playoffs, when he made what appeared to be a sensational touchdown catch over a Green Bay defender, only to have the score overturned because officials ruled that Bryant didn't maintain possession of the ball as he hit the ground and rolled into the end zone—even though the ball never touched the turf. The Cowboys lost that game 26–21, and the ruling on that catch/noncatch sparked enough controversy to be named the Dez Bryant rule. The rule has since been overturned, but the memory of plays like that still haunt the game.

Since then, all manner of should-have-been catches have been ruled incomplete. It happened to the Steelers in week fifteen, when Ben Roethlisberger hit Jesse James in the end zone with less than a minute left in the fourth to give the Steelers what would have been a win over—you guessed it—the Patriots. James caught the ball and fell into the end zone, and just as the ball hit the ground, it shifted in his hands. He never lost control, but the officials ruled it incomplete. Like the Cowboys before them, the Steelers ended up losing the game.

I had a completion overturned in Kansas City myself, when I threw a thirty-seven-yarder to Travis Kelce. He caught it, took two steps, and dove out of bounds at the one yard line. The ball hit the ground, and then he fumbled it out of bounds. It was obviously a catch, but it was called incomplete. Like I said, there are no guarantees in the NFL.

It felt like an eternity as we waited for Gene Steratore to come out of that reviewing booth and render a decision. When he finally came out and announced, "The ruling on the field stands," the crowd went crazy. So did we. All up and down the sideline, the guys were high-fiving and hugging each other.

Our celebration didn't last long, though. The game was far from over. After my two-point conversion pass attempt to Corey failed, the score remained 38–33. There was still 2:21 left on the clock, and Brady was about to get the ball, trailing by five.

HOLDING OUR BREATH

There's a reason Tom Brady has five Super Bowl titles. With all the fourth-quarter comebacks he has led, you can never count him out.

When the game is on the line and the ball is in his hands, everyone expects him to do something special. That's the reputation he has created for himself.

Already that night, he had thrown for more than 450 yards, with three touchdowns and no interceptions. That's pretty impressive. However, so was our defense. They hadn't gotten nearly as much credit as our offense throughout the year, but our entire defensive unit, from coordinator Jim Schwartz down to the last player, was a force to be reckoned with. And with the game in the balance, they came up with one of the biggest plays of the year.

On second and two from the New England thirty-three, our line quickly collapsed the pocket. Defensive end Brandon Graham, an eight-year veteran and our season sacks leader with nine and a half, bulled his way forward from an interior line position to strip the ball from Brady's hand and register a sack. Not only that, but the ball bounced right into the hands of fellow end Derek Barnett (a rookie first-round draft pick), giving us the ball back—and handing us control of the game clock.

From there, the goal was to score while burning as much of the clock as possible. We called three straight run plays for LeGarrette to put Jake into field goal range, and then he nailed a forty-six-yard attempt, making the score 41–33.

That field goal was huge. Yes, New England got the ball back with fifty-eight seconds left on the clock, but they couldn't win it in regulation. The best they could do would be to force an overtime with a touchdown and a two-point conversion. The pressure was on them. Still, crazier things have happened.

Brady quickly got to work. He threw three straight incomplete passes before finally connecting with Danny Amendola for thirteen yards, bringing the Patriots to their own twenty-two. But the clock was their enemy. Brady rushed to the line and spiked the ball with twenty-six seconds left. Two more passes to Gronk brought them to midfield, but with just nine seconds left and no time-outs remaining, they had only one realistic option: a Hail Mary.

Though virtually every player on the Patriots offense is a threat, all fingers pointed to the final throw going to Gronk in the end zone. When the ball was snapped, Brandon came streaking around the left edge and almost registered a game-ending sack, but Brady managed to wriggle free, step into the pocket, and launch a prayer. In the end zone, six defensive backs circled Gronk like buzzards. Danny Amendola and fellow receiver Phillip Dorsett trailed a few steps behind Gronk, jockeying for position in case of a rebound, and as the ball bounced off one set of fingertips after another, our entire team held its collective breath. For a split second, it looked like one of them might have a shot.

It's going to be Amendola. It's always Amendola.

Then, in the blink of an eye, the ball hit the ground. All game, I'd been telling myself not to pay attention to the clock. But at that moment, I looked up and saw those big, bright digits on the scoreboard: 0:00.

I did a quick scan of the field. No flags. It was all over. 41–33.

First came shock. Then celebration. And finally all-out pandemonium.

We had done it.

We were officially Super Bowl champions.

CHAPTER 14

PHINALLY

Once Tom Brady's Hail Mary pass bounced harmlessly off the turf, I put my hands on my head and gazed ahead, stunned. Then the emotional dam inside me cracked open, releasing a torrent of feelings that had been building for weeks.

All the sacrifice and hard work you put in over an entire season leads to this one moment, and when it finally happens, the emotions can't help but spill over. It was finally starting to sink in that we'd just beat what many considered an unbeatable opponent on the biggest stage in American sports. As a football player, you spend so much of your time preparing for games. But no one tells you how to prepare for the emotions of a Super Bowl victory.

Apparently, another dam also burst at that moment—the one restraining roughly a zillion media members. By the time I got onto the field to celebrate with my teammates, it was so packed I could barely move. Reporters, photographers, cameramen, NFL personnel, and security were everywhere. It was like Broad Street after the NFC championship game—times a hundred.

You'd think getting to midfield to shake hands with the Patriots would have been a relatively simple task, but it wasn't. Nothing was easy in that mob scene.

My senses were on overload. Players and coaches were running around embracing one another. Lights were flashing from all directions. Streamers and Lombardi Trophy–shaped confetti were raining down from the sky as though a giant piñata had just exploded overhead. And it was so noisy you practically had to scream to be heard.

I thought about Eagles fans and what this meant to them and the city of Philadelphia. Generations of fans had come and gone, eagerly waiting for a Super Bowl championship. Finally, the wait was over.

I managed to find several of my teammates, hug them, and share a brief moment together. Almost twenty minutes passed before I was able to find Tori, Lily, and my mom standing behind a roped-off area for players' family members. Tori and I embraced, kissed, and just stared at each other for a long time. We could hardly come up with any words for a moment like that one.

I couldn't help but think back to that night on the porch with Tori a year and a half earlier, when we talked, prayed, and sought God's will for my career. Despite all my fears and doubts, she had patiently encouraged me to give football one more shot, believing that God still had a purpose for me in the NFL—and she was 100 percent correct.

I can't thank God enough for Tori. My view was shortsighted during that time, but she was able to see things clearly, viewing it all through the lens of faith and love. She never gave up on me.

I eventually broke the silence with a tongue-in-cheek apology. "I'm sorry," I said with a smirk. "Our lives just changed a little bit."

It was the second time in as many weeks that I'd had that realization—the first being the standing ovation in the restaurant before I left for Minneapolis, and now here. Nothing ever would be the same for us again, and all joking aside, I honestly didn't know how to feel about that.

Tori and I are both pretty reserved by nature. We don't actively seek out attention. When the spotlight shines in my direction, I can deal with it, but it doesn't come naturally. I'm used to walking around in California during the off-season and being completely unnoticed. Even in Philadelphia, I was able to go unrecognized until fairly recently.

As the confetti continued to rain down and one teammate after another made their way past me to meet up with their families, I flashed back to the pregame warm-up interview snafu, and a funny thought crossed my mind: *I should probably try to find Nate and apologize for changing his life too. Or at the very least, I should suggest that he grow a beard.*

A STAR IS BORN

As the time approached for the Lombardi Trophy presentation, a security official came up to me and asked if I'd like to take my daughter onstage.

Nineteen months earlier, when I'd contemplated walking away from football, one of my biggest regrets was that I'd always dreamed of sharing my career with my kids, but at the time, Tori and I didn't have any children. Then God gave us Lily. I wasn't sure how she'd react to all the chaos, but I did know one thing—there was no way I was going to celebrate this moment without her.

"Yes, let's bring her up," I said. "I want my daughter to be here with me."

Lily looked adorable dressed up in her little jean jacket with "Foles" on the back and wearing her pink noise-canceling headphones. Not only was she not frightened, but she had the time of her life up there. She pawed at the microphone during my interview with Dan Patrick and stared at the confetti coming down. She was a perfectly content little angel, blissfully unaware of the football history being made around her. And even though at seven months old she was too young to appreciate it, it meant the world to me to have her up there. She had helped keep me grounded throughout the entire season, and she provided the perspective I needed in that moment.

In retrospect, I probably should have apologized to Lily that night too, because the next day, the Internet exploded with pictures and articles about her. Forget that Foles guy—she was the *real* star of the show. And that was fine by me.

The Lombardi Trophy represents the pinnacle of football. As a kid, you dream about hoisting it over your head, and you obsess over it as an adult. I'm not going to lie—it felt great to hold that shiny silver trophy in my hands. But at the end of the day, it didn't even come close to the joy I felt holding Lily for the first time. My team may have won the Super Bowl, and I may have just been named MVP, but getting to be Lily's dad topped all that.

I know Lily will never remember those chaotic few moments she spent with me on the podium that night, but someday when we dig out the scrapbook and she asks about the picture of me hoisting the Lombardi, I'll look at her with pride and say, "Just so you know, the real trophy in my arms that night was you."

LASTING MEMORIES

Because the NFL tries to manage the hullabaloo slightly by only allowing a few family members on the field at a time, I hadn't seen my dad yet. Then, as Coach Pederson and I were waiting to do our NFL Network interview, I spotted some of our family members and friends standing off to the side.

I tapped my dad on the shoulder, and when he turned around, I gave him a gigantic hug. "I knew you could do this," he said. "I always believed you would." For Dad, getting to attend the Super Bowl in person would have been exciting enough. But he got to see his son perform on that stage—and win. I know he was living and dying with every play, so it meant a lot to both of us to share that moment.

After the NFL Network interview, I was able to steal away to the locker room for a few moments of . . . more crowds. It was almost as though the field had been moved indoors. There were reporters everywhere. Many of my teammates had already showered and put on their street clothes and were getting ready to go to the after-party.

I tracked down Nate, Carson, and Spencer Phillips and gave each of them a hug. To avoid the throng, we slipped into the training room. Zach Ertz, Mark Lewis (the team's assistant athletic trainer, who helped me rehab my arm during the preseason), and a few other guys were there too. For twenty minutes we enjoyed a peaceful respite, chatted about the game, and marveled at the journey God had brought us on.

Not surprisingly, Carson handled the entire evening with dignity and grace. The game had to have been bittersweet for him. He was an enormous part of our success, starting the first thirteen games and positioning us perfectly for the NFC East title. After his injury, he provided constant encouragement and insight. I know he wanted to be on the field that day. He's a quarterback, after all, and quarterbacks want to be in the huddle. They want to feel the pressure. That's just how we're wired. Yet Carson's joy was genuine. Before we all split up for the evening, I made sure to remind him that we wouldn't have been there without him and his leadership. It's safe to say that every guy in that room felt the same way.

Before we left, Tony Dungy came in with his youngest son, Jordan, to offer his congratulations. I've always admired Tony, not only because of what he has accomplished as a coach but also because of the kind of man he is. Tony is a strong Christian who never compromises when it comes to his faith. In fact, it's the cornerstone of everything he does. The league is full of guys like Tony—solid, honest, hardworking guys who look for every opportunity to live out their faith, impact others, and glorify God.

Tori, Lily, Carson, Nate, Zach, Tony, our family, and our friends— I couldn't imagine a better group of people to celebrate one of the greatest nights of my life with.

A TALE OF TWO AFTER-PARTIES

You'd think a Super Bowl after-party would be a pretty cool scene, right? Well, yes and no. I guess it depends on what you're looking for in an after-party.

The official event was held at a hotel near the stadium. I wanted to hang out for a while with my teammates, enjoy their company, and bask in our victory. We'd created a special atmosphere within the locker room that year, and these guys were like family to me. I was hoping to soak up a little more time with them, figuring we'd be able to talk and savor memories from the game and the season.

Boy, was I wrong.

I had assumed the event would be for players, coaches, and immediate family members only. But when I arrived, there were tons of other people there too—friends, extended family members, former players, former coaches, you name it. Tori had gone back to the Radisson Blu with our families, and she planned to come to the party after putting Lily down for the night. After only a few minutes, however, I was starting to wish I'd gone to the hotel with them. I could barely move. It felt like the postgame scene at the stadium, just packed into a smaller space. It was a claustrophobic's worst nightmare.

Everybody was talking so loudly that I couldn't even hear myself think. Everywhere I turned, people were grabbing me to take selfies, shaking my hand, and slapping me on the back. It was a lot to navigate, especially considering that my fuel tank was pretty much empty by that point.

I finally spotted Frank Reich and his wife, Linda, across the room and went to chat with them for a few minutes. I hadn't had a chance to connect with Frank after the game, and I was eager to thank him for everything he'd done for me that season. I will always be grateful for the amazing mentor and friend Frank has been to me. Hearing about his journey of attending seminary while being a player inspired me as I planned to go to seminary myself.

After a few minutes, we were joined by Trey Burton and Patrick Robinson, who were as ready as I was to leave and spend time with their families. So after we said good-bye to Frank and Linda, the three of us escaped into the extreme Minnesota cold, wearing nothing but our dress clothes. In Minneapolis. In February.

It was the coldest Super Bowl on record, and there we were—three guys from Philadelphia, all walking around in just our sport coats. Go figure.

Since none of us had a car, we arranged for an Uber pickup. When we got in the car, the driver took one look at us and asked, "You guys want the heat on?"

We just looked at each other and laughed. "Yeah, we want the heat on! It's negative ten outside!" Only in Minnesota.

When we got back to the Radisson Blu, the place was deserted, so I got to spend about an hour visiting with my family—no crowds, no cameras, no chaos. It was perfect. Despite my exhaustion, it was wonderful to be able to reflect on everything God had done for us over the past several months. My brothers-in-law, Ryan and Evan, were both there, and we reminisced about that August evening when I called them to say I was giving football another shot and to recruit them as late-night throwing partners.

"Just think about it," Ryan said. "A year and a half ago, we were at a random park at nine o'clock at night throwing a football around to help you get ready to go to Kansas City. Now here you are—a Super Bowl champion."

We all shook our heads and laughed. What else could we do? It was all so improbable. How do you go from almost stepping away from the game to winning the Super Bowl in eighteen months? That kind of thing just doesn't happen. Then again, as I'd come to discover time and time again—first with Tori's illness, then in Kansas City, and then back in Philly—"with God everything is possible" (Matthew 19:26).

But all good things must also come to an end, even on Super Bowl Sunday. Eventually, someone reminded me that I had a press conference early the next morning, so I excused myself and went back to my room to get some sleep. By the time my head hit the pillow, it was just after 4 a.m. My press conference was scheduled for 8 a.m. Exhausted as I was, my mind was still racing. I wouldn't get much sleep that night, but hey, at least the heat was on.

MOST VALUABLE MOMENT

The alarm clock went off at 6:30 a.m., sounding like a banshee's wail. I dragged myself out of bed, hopped into the shower, made a quick cup of coffee, got dressed, and just barely made it to my press conference in time. No suit and tie this time, just a T-shirt, a Super Bowl hat, and a Super Bowl jacket. I didn't even have time to shave. It's hard to know what the dress code is for events you've never been to, and since this was my first Super Bowl MVP press conference, I decided to just come as me. Happily, Roger Goodell, who presented the award, also opted for casual that morning. Solidarity.

I tried to remain as coherent as possible during the brief Q and A, but I was still feeling a little groggy.

As expected, the first question had to do with how surprised everyone was at my performance over the past four weeks. I couldn't blame them. I was pretty amazed myself to be standing at the podium fielding questions as a Super Bowl MVP. But I think there's a difference between being amazed and being surprised. In my mind, amazement is the natural awestruck response that comes from bearing witness to something truly extraordinary. Surprise, on the other hand, implies that you didn't believe it was possible in the first place. I never doubted that this moment was possible. Not because I thought I was the greatest quarterback who ever lived, but because of the incredibly talented players and coaching staff who had been beside me the whole time.

Football is and always will be a team sport. And as honored and humbled as I was to be selected as MVP, the truth is, I almost felt a little guilty receiving it. I never would have been there without the help of Doug, Frank, Spencer, Press, Carson, Nate, Zach, Corey, Alshon, Jay, LeGarrette, Nelson, Trey, and everyone else on the team.

That's why when I accepted the award, I did it on behalf of the entire Eagles organization.

No one gets to that podium by himself, and even though I was dead tired, I was incredibly grateful to have had the opportunity to shine a much-deserved spotlight on my coaches and teammates. At the end of the day, that's what it's all about—the way we care about and support one another professionally, emotionally, and spiritually.

THE MOST MAGICAL PLACE ON EARTH

As soon as the press conference was over, I went back to the hotel, packed up my stuff, and rounded up Tori, Lily, and our moms for the next event on the post–Super Bowl itinerary. You guessed it—we were going to Disney World!

I was running on fumes, but even so, I couldn't sleep on the way to Orlando. There was still so much adrenaline coursing through my body, and I was trying to take in everything that had happened. Considering how messed up her schedule had been the past few days, Lily was a champ on the plane. As soon as we arrived, I jumped on a float and took part in a thirty-minute parade down Main Street USA, accompanied by none other than Mickey himself.

In retrospect, the cast of characters I found myself rubbing elbows with over the course of just thirty-six hours was pretty extraordinary— first Tom Brady and Bill Belichick, then Roger Goodell and Tony Dungy, and now Mickey Mouse. It's hard to top that.

It was incredible to see how many Eagles fans attended the parade. There were thousands of fans there—it was a sea of green. I expected that there would be a massive turnout when we got back home in a few days, but I had no idea so many people would turn up in Florida.

I mean, the Super Bowl was less than twenty-four hours ago. When had these people booked their tickets? That's what I call faith.

Tori, Lily, my mom, and Tori's mom went to a VIP area to watch the rest of the parade while my agent and I took off for Big Thunder Mountain Railroad and Pandora, the 3-D ride from the movie *Avatar*. Before we left, my mom warned me, "You always get sick on virtual-reality rides."

"No, I don't!" I said, with all the bravado a grown man being scolded by his mother at Disney World can muster.

Two minutes into the ride, I was sure I was going to throw up. What can I say? Moms know best.

Then it was time to go to the airport and head back to Philly. What a whirlwind—we left Minneapolis at 9:30 a.m. and got back home around 10:30 p.m. It was a long, fun (and only occasionally nauseating) day.

GREEN AROUND THE PHILS

Speaking of nausea, by Thursday of that week, whether it was from a virus or sheer physical exhaustion, I woke up feeling miserable— vomiting and everything. If it were any other day, I would have stayed in bed. But there was no way I was going to miss the Eagles' championship parade through downtown Philadelphia!

Everyone met at Lincoln Finanical Field. After checking in, I asked a security guy to let me into the locker room so I could lie down for a little bit and see if I could get my stomach under control. For about ninety minutes, I just lay in front of my locker and chatted with Nate and Spencer.

By the time we had to start boarding the buses, the temperature was in the twenties and really windy. Just what the doctor ordered for a guy suffering from nausea and chills. I was completely exhausted and feeling wretched, but it was a Super Bowl parade—the stuff you dream about. I was determined to enjoy it as much as possible.

Flu symptoms aside, being at the front of the big bus with Carson, Nate, and Jeffrey Lurie, the team owner, was incredible. And it was an amazing experience to hoist the Lombardi Trophy from atop the bus for all the fans to see. After all, a lot of them had been waiting for this moment since before I was even born.

As we made our way down Broad Street, I saw so much joy in people's faces. Entire generations of families were out there in the freezing weather, waving, screaming, and having a great time.

At certain points along the route, fans threw beer cans at the parade vehicles. If you're thinking this was a sign of anger or disrespect, you don't know the City of Brotherly Love. These fans were hoping we'd catch the beer and drink it. They were flinging alcoholic beverages at us in a supportive, Philly kind of way.

When I think of the Philly fan base, there's one incident from my rookie season that sums it up for me. In December of 2012, I drove into the city to have dinner with fellow quarterback Trent Edwards at his downtown condo. The next morning we were leaving for Dallas, where I would make my third career start in the Sunday night game. Finding parking in downtown Philly is difficult and fairly expensive, so I parked on the side of the street, not realizing it was reserved for motorcycles. Two hours later, when I came back, my car was gone.

Uh-oh.

I walked to the impound lot and waited in line until after 1 a.m. to get my vehicle out. I was sober, but other patrons there couldn't say the same. Eventually, someone recognized me.

"Hey, aren't you Nick Foles?"

"Yeah."

The staff all gathered around and then brought me to their back offices. We started to chat, and they told me their stories. They were hardworking, blue-collar folks—old-school Philly folks. Some of them were season ticket holders. They worked their tails off just to make ends meet and take their families to the games. Eagles fandom was woven into the fabric of their lives, passed down from previous generations. I took photos with them and signed some autographs.

"Well," I finally said, "you know we have a game on Sunday. I need to get going."

"Oh yeah!" They scurried off to get my truck.

Sweet, I thought. *It's all been a misunderstanding, an honest mistake—rookie quarterback in town trying to figure out how to park in Philly.* After all that time chatting, I was sure they'd let the payment slide.

Then they pulled up with my truck.

"Okay, Nick," the guy said. "That'll be $350."

Dang. No perks.

These folks loved the Eagles, but $350 is $350. Folks have to earn a living. That's Philly.

I'm sure every team feels this way, but I really do believe we have the best fans in the world. In spite of the bad rap they get sometimes, they love their team with all their hearts, and win or lose, they always show a tremendous amount of support. People who have never been to Philly always ask me—especially after years like 2012, when we went 4–12—"Were the fans all over you? Did you have to walk around with a bodyguard?" The answer is no—never. I've never had any problems walking around the city. Eagles fans are fervent, and just like any other fan base, they don't like it when their team loses. But they always have our backs. They're always at the stadium in force—loud, proud, and ready to roll.

Whenever I run into fans in public—whether it's at an autograph signing, outside the stadium, or even in California during the off-season—they have nothing but positive things to say to me. In the months following the Super Bowl, I couldn't believe how many people approached me with tears as they shared their own stories. I remember one guy in his early thirties whose mother had just died of cancer. He said she'd waited her entire life to watch the Eagles win the Super Bowl. Before she passed away, she saw the game, and it gave her great happiness.

From the moment I set foot in Philadelphia, I could sense that the fans were starved for a championship. And now, to be part of something that provided so much joy to people made everything worth it—the sweat, the training, the hard work, the sacrifice, and even the injuries. Very few players get to experience winning a Super Bowl, let alone doing so for a community as invested as Philly is. I feel blessed to have been part of this victory for the whole city.

As the parade continued, the buses looped around City Hall and made their way up Benjamin Franklin Parkway to the Philadelphia Museum of Art, home of the famous Rocky statue that commemorates the scene in the film where Rocky Balboa climbs the steps as part of his training. The fact that the parade route ended at the Rocky steps seemed appropriate. Rocky was an underdog too.

More than our underdog status, though, what I'll most remember about the 2017 Eagles is our belief in and love for one another. So many people doubted us, but we kept ignoring the outside noise, and we came away with a huge victory when it mattered most. It was really special to be a part of something like that.

At the museum, we were greeted by the biggest crowd I've ever seen in my life—and keep in mind, I'd just come back from the Super Bowl and Disney World. *The only thing that would make this better is if Tori and Lily were here with me,* I thought.

That morning Tori and I had discussed whether she and Lily should ride with me on the bus. Tori really wanted to come, but I knew it was going to be a long, cold day, and I didn't want Lily to be out in that weather and risk getting what I had, so I convinced Tori to stay at home with my mom and my mother-in-law.

Imagine my surprise when we got onstage and I saw Tori, my mom, and Lily sitting right in the front row! Even though the main roads had been shut down and roped off for the parade, Tori called our team's head of security, who worked with the local police to get them across town to the museum in time for our speeches.

That's my girl.

And that's the City of Brotherly Love.

ENCORE WITH MICKEY

Once the clamor of the Super Bowl and all the postgame celebrations dissipated, I did what I always try to do after a game—I called my grandfather, Mickey. Only this time, Grandad didn't ask any questions about my playing time. He was thrilled beyond words at what had transpired in the Super Bowl. I could practically see his smile through the phone.

He and some other family members had gotten together at his brother Mike's house to watch Super Bowl LII. They also DVRed it, and by the time I called, Mickey and Mike had probably rewatched it three or four times.

In many ways, our post–Super Bowl conversation wasn't much different from our other talks.

"Nick!" he exclaimed. "You did so good! We had so much fun watching you."

"So you enjoyed the game?"

"Oh yes, I really enjoyed it."

That was about it—short and simple, but filled with so much love.

He ended the conversation the same way he always does: "Well, call me back soon."

Whether I'm the Super Bowl MVP or a guy who just got traded, I know Grandad is proud of me. I'm his grandson, and he loves me simply as Nick—with or without the career accomplishments. That has never changed.

And no matter what the future holds, it never will.

CHAPTER 15

BE STILL AND KNOW

Every great story has a sequel. Mine was ushered in on the tail of a burning question that everyone wanted to know: Would Nick Foles become the first Super Bowl MVP to start the following season as a backup?

In the fifty-two-year history of the Super Bowl, there has never been another quarterback who has won Super Bowl MVP and then started the next season on the bench.

Until me.

When I signed my contract with the Eagles in 2017, I agreed to a two-year deal, so I belong to the Eagles until they decide to trade me or my contract expires at the end of the 2018 season.

This didn't come as a surprise. Even as we were standing atop the Rocky steps waving to the crowd, I knew full well that as soon as Carson was cleared to play, he'd return to the starting role, whether it was the first game of the season or the tenth.

The media knew it too. Cleanup crews had barely finished sweeping up the confetti when the Internet and airwaves started humming with discussions about my future:

"The Eagles should trade Foles while his value is sky high. Nothing less than two first-round draft picks will do!"

"The Eagles should keep Foles for insurance until Carson Wentz returns from injury."

"Any other team would die for a Super Bowl MVP as a backup!"

What the media didn't know, however, was what's in my heart. What they saw as a riches-to-rags sports story, I see as part of God's divine plan. I've said all along that my desire is to play for God's glory, not mine, and that's exactly what I plan to do.

My unique path from backup to Super Bowl MVP to backup again is a powerful message to share with people, and God has given me an ideal platform to do that from. To cheerfully return to a backup role after reaching the pinnacle of the sport contradicts everything the world tells us about success, fame, money, and self-worth. To me, it's a tangible reminder that we are called to humility and to a life of service. As Scripture puts it, "Don't think you are better than you really are. Be honest in your evaluation of yourselves, measuring yourselves by the faith God has given us" (Romans 12:3).

Some people might think I deserve a better deal, but it's not about what I deserve. It's never been about that. The truth is, I've already been given far more than I deserve—a wonderful family; a job I love; grace and forgiveness; great friends, coaches, and teammates. Everything I have is a gift from God, and I'm thankful for all of it. I am where I am right now because of God's grace, and I'll continue to follow wherever he leads.

If an opportunity arises at some point to go to a team that's a good fit for our family, Tori and I would be open to it. In fact, several teams inquired about trading for me, but in the end, none of the offers fit what the Eagles were looking for. Who knows—maybe one of those trades would have given me the opportunity to have a starting role somewhere else and impact another team. But being traded just for the sake of being traded is not my end goal.

Tori and I both love Philadelphia—the city, the fans, the organization. While I am eager to have a team invest in me as their leader, I know God is in control, and if that's his will, the opportunity will present itself at the right time. Football is my calling now, and if God wants us in Philly for the time being, then that's where we'll be. I'll strive to glorify him, remain humble, and focus on having a positive impact on others—just like I would anywhere else.

That doesn't mean it's always easy. It was hard to watch other players—quarterbacks in particular—sign massive contracts in the weeks following the Super Bowl. On a daily basis, I have to fight the internal battle to keep my priorities straight. My near-constant prayer following the Super Bowl has been, "God, you are greater than all of this. I need to stop trying to do everything in my own power and just trust you. If you don't want me to play football anymore, I need to honor you in that, too."

That last part about not playing football anymore is by far the toughest. I don't know what the future holds. It's possible I might not play a single snap in 2018—or ever again. And if that's God's will, I can live with that. But I hope it's not.

I'm not perfect—far from it. Pride, envy, and selfishness work their way into my heart just like they do in everyone else. That's why I rely so heavily on God's Word. Reading the Bible helps me recenter myself when I start to spin out of control. One of the most meaningful passages of Scripture I meditated on during the 2018 off-season was Matthew 6:25-34, a beautiful portion of Jesus' famous Sermon on the Mount:

> That is why I tell you not to worry about everyday life—whether you have enough food and drink, or enough clothes to wear. Isn't life more than food, and your body more than clothing? Look at the birds. They don't plant or harvest or store food in barns, for your heavenly Father feeds them. And aren't you far more valuable to him than they are? Can all your worries add a single moment to your life?
>
> And why worry about your clothing? Look at the lilies of the field and how they grow. They don't work or make their clothing, yet Solomon in all his glory was not dressed as beautifully as they are. And if God cares so wonderfully for wildflowers that are here today and thrown into the fire tomorrow, he will certainly care for you. Why do you have so little faith?
>
> So don't worry about these things, saying, "What will we eat? What will we drink? What will we wear?" These things dominate the thoughts of unbelievers, but your heavenly Father already knows all your needs. Seek the Kingdom of God above all else, and live righteously, and he will give you everything you need.
>
> So don't worry about tomorrow, for tomorrow will bring its own worries. Today's trouble is enough for today.

In other words, "Stop worrying, Nick. God loves you, and he will take care of all your needs."

This is the attitude I constantly try to maintain. If I start basing my career decisions on pride, fame, money, or personal glory, then it's time to step away, because I've taken God out of the driver's seat and put the focus on me. And nothing good can come from that.

It's so easy for your heart to slip in this business. And for me, the 2018 off-season was more difficult than most. Agents were constantly calling with updates on potential trade offers, which posed their own challenges, because I started to ask myself questions like, *Well, what would I play for?* or *How much am I worth?* or *Is that enough?* I needed to constantly remind myself that God didn't give me my football skills to make me rich; he gave them to me so I could serve and honor him.

Tori and I talked about this struggle almost daily during the 2018 off-season. As the phone calls came in, trade deadlines whizzed by, and starting quarterback slots got filled throughout the league, we tried to remain focused on God and his plan for us.

We don't know what lies ahead for us, but we do know this: "God causes everything to work together for the good of those who love God and are called according to his purpose for them" (Romans 8:28). So for now, we just have to remain faithful and wait until God reveals his plan.

After the Super Bowl, I had to acknowledge that God had written an amazing story to bring me this far. Now I have to trust him with the next chapter of my life. He's big enough to handle this, too.

Of course, distractions are inevitable. But when I step back and consider what God has done in my life, I can't help but be grateful, and that keeps me grounded.

Near the end of Psalm 46, God says to the psalmist, "Be still, and know that I am God." Well, that's where Tori and I are right now.

Being still.

Knowing.

And waiting.

ONCE AN EAGLE . . .

If and when the time comes, it will be hard to leave Philadelphia, because part of me will always be an Eagle. There's just something special about the passion of Philadelphia fans. You feed off of it. That's why you play the game. When you play in a city like Philly and don that midnight green, playing becomes more than a job. It becomes an integral part of you. You develop a deep affection for the team, the fans, and the city itself.

The longer you play in the league, the more you realize how fleeting success is. Guys can play their entire careers and never even make it to the playoffs, let alone win a Super Bowl. To create a cohesive, family atmosphere like we did with the 2017 Eagles—and become world champions, to boot—is something truly special. That's why the thought of someday leaving it—whether to go to another team or to walk away and do something else entirely—is difficult for Tori and me.

I know that every day I get to play in the NFL is a blessing, but even so, I don't want to play until I'm forty-five. After my two-year agreement with the Eagles expires at the end of the 2018 season, Tori and I will sit down and talk about where our hearts are. We want to make sure we're staying in the NFL for the right reasons. As long as we feel that my staying in football will glorify God, we'll continue to do it. But if there comes a day when we don't feel that way, we've agreed that it will be time for me to step away.

Thanks to my experience in the wilderness in 2016, I now know that I can retire at any time and be truly happy. It's not that time yet, but I'll know when it is. It takes a lot of faith to play this game, and I fully believe that God will give me enough faith to know when it's over too.

MOSES AND ME

The question I'm asked more than any other these days is, "Aren't you glad you made the decision to come back to football?"

Of course! I'm very happy I made that decision. But even if I hadn't come back, it wouldn't have necessarily been a mistake. I think that's where some people get confused. It was never a matter of right or wrong; it was a decision of faith. If I had retired in 2016, my life wouldn't have ended. I still would have had a purpose to fulfill. I simply would have moved on to something else, believing that God could use me there, too.

When I hang up my cleats someday, one of the things I really want to do is work with kids. I would like to bring the message of eternal hope and significance to the next generation. There are plenty of people out there who say things like, "If you work hard, you'll achieve your goals." I've probably heard that speech a thousand times myself. But all it did was make me feel like a failure if I didn't reach certain objectives. What resonated with me the most was when successful people spoke about their failures and how they overcame them. That's what gave me the incentive to work hard—knowing that it was okay to fail.

Now that God has placed me in a position of influence, I want to share my own journey—warts and all—with people. I love football, but football isn't my first love. God is, then my family. Football comes after that. And because I have that perspective, I'm a much better player than I was before.

So many kids are taught early on that football is everything and that they have to be the best. I want to help them change that mindset so they can see that football is just one piece of a larger, more significant life. You don't have to *be* the best in order to *do* your best.

It's all about where your heart is. If kids can reorient their priorities early on, not only will they be better football players when they get older, but they'll have more fulfilled lives overall. Their joy and their identities won't be based solely on their athletic performance like mine used to be, but rather on their relationships with Christ and their family—the things that will last long after football is over.

During the 2017 off-season, I visited a local chapter of the Fellowship of Christian Athletes in Philadelphia and shared my faith story with the teenagers there. I know I would have benefited from that type of spiritual guidance at that age, and I enjoyed connecting with the students. In fact, I've been thinking a lot about becoming a youth pastor after I retire from football. That's part of the reason I'm pursuing an online seminary degree. I don't necessarily want to become a lead pastor, but I definitely want to get more involved in my local church and help kids and teens navigate life's complexities.

I'm open to where God leads me, although I have to admit my interests and gifts are more suited to connecting with people one-on-one or in small group situations than to speaking to large groups. Public speaking and I enjoy a cordial relationship, but we're not best pals. I am getting more comfortable addressing a crowd, but it's not something I always dreamed of doing. Truth be told, when it comes to public speaking, I kind of feel a connection to Moses.

When God called Moses to go to Egypt and tell Pharaoh to free the Israelites from slavery, Moses wasn't too keen on the idea, and he tried to get out of it. "O Lord," he said, "I'm not very good with words. I never have been, and I'm not now, even though you have spoken to me. I get tongue-tied, and my words get tangled" (Exodus 4:10).

I can relate, brother.

Unfortunately, Moses was arguing with the wrong guy. God—who, for the record, is a phenomenal public speaker—said, "Who makes a person's mouth? Who decides whether people speak or do not speak, hear or do not hear, see or do not see? Is it not I, the LORD? Now go! I will be with you as you speak, and I will instruct you in what to say" (Exodus 4:11-12). With God's help, Moses did just fine. And with God's help, so will I.

I don't know what life after football will hold for me. Trying to predict the future is pointless. It would be like a football coach trying to script out every detail for the fourth quarter before the game even starts and expecting everything to play out as planned. We can't know what will happen to us tomorrow or a month from now, let alone in five years. Only God knows what lies ahead.

Whenever I think I have a firm grasp on where my future is headed, God usually shows me a different—and better—plan. Whenever I say, "This is what I think will happen," God stretches me in ways I can't even fathom. He doesn't promise that we'll be comfortable; in fact, he often does his best work when we're stretched beyond what we think we can do.

God loves to take our small dreams and expand them into jaw-dropping realities that are worthy of his divine glory. So I've stopped trying to grip the future like the laces on a football. Instead, I'm trying to move forward in faith, holding my plans loosely.

CHAPTER 16

DON'T CALL ME SUPERMAN

I'm not sure why you read this book or why you're interested in the story of my career thus far or what happened to the 2017 Philadelphia Eagles in general.

My guess is that somewhere along the way you were inspired. Something about how that season unfolded moved you. Whether it was the narrative of my life or my teammates' lives or our team as a whole, something stirred your heart. If so, you're not alone. I feel the same way. The 2017 season changed me forever—not because I can now call myself a Super Bowl champion, but because of the powerful lessons God taught me along the way.

When people look back at our remarkable Super Bowl run—whether it's a year from now or twenty—I think they'll still be asking, "How did that happen?" Even now, it hardly seems real. In fact, there's a fairy-tale-like quality about it.

But it did happen. Among many other things, our 2017 season was a celebration of the impossible—a drama played out in real time, showing just how far a team can go when they believe in a common goal, when they bond together, when they push through adversity, and when they play courageously right down to the last man.

Our journey featured all the story lines and plot twists that great drama requires:

- A historic franchise seeks its first-ever Super Bowl victory and first NFL title in fifty-seven years.
- An impressive collection of talented individuals comes together, forsaking personal glory, to accomplish the unforgettable.
- A team races out of the gate despite key injuries early on, led by a bright young star who has "franchise quarterback" written all over him.
- As the playoffs near, disaster strikes when the MVP-caliber quarterback suffers a season-ending injury, causing most folks to reconsider the team's chances.
- A veteran backup who had considered retirement two years before steps in, struggles early, then leads the team to a world championship over the greatest dynasty the sport has ever seen.
- A long-suffering city that fully embraces its gritty, underdog *Rocky* ethos celebrates its long-awaited crown.

Who would have believed that script? Only a few. But we played it out—improv theater on a grand scale—and it was magnificent.

Perhaps, though, you started reading this book because you were inspired in a different way. Maybe as you glimpsed my story, you saw a person like yourself—someone who struggles daily. Someone who doesn't have all the answers. Someone who has failed many times and says, "Failing is okay. But what am I supposed to learn from it?"

Whatever the reason you picked up this book, my hope is that you've been inspired by what I consider to be one of my life's greatest themes: the immense power and potential of human weakness. It sounds contradictory and even absurd—the power of weakness—but it's also beautifully and mysteriously true.

I'm living proof.

STRENGTH IN WEAKNESS

During my MVP press conference, a Philadelphia TV reporter asked me what I'd like people to take away from my unique journey. At that particular moment, I was running on fumes. The night before, I'd gotten a ragged two-and-a-half hours of sleep. Plus, I still had a long day ahead of me. Physically speaking, I didn't feel like I had the energy to share anything terribly valuable. But when the reporter asked that question, my response came straight from the heart. Here's what I said:

I think the big thing is, don't be afraid to fail. In our
society today—Instagram, Twitter—it's a highlight reel.
It's all the good things. . . . And then when you have a
rough day or your life's not [as] good as that, [you think]
you're failing. Failure's a part of life. [It's] a part of building
character and growing. Without failure, who would you
be? I wouldn't be up here if I hadn't fallen thousands of
times, made mistakes. We all are human; we all have
weaknesses. Throughout this, being able to share that and

be transparent [is important]. I know when I listen to people speak and they share their weaknesses, I'm listening because I can resonate. I'm not perfect. I'm not Superman. I might be in the NFL, and we might have just won the Super Bowl, but hey, we still have daily struggles. I still have daily struggles. But that's where my faith comes in. That's where my family comes in. I think when you look at a struggle in your life, just know that's an opportunity for your character to grow. That's really just been the message. It's simple: if something's going on in your life and you're struggling, embrace it because you're growing.

Apparently that portion of the interview went viral. Stories started popping up all over the Internet, and it created a buzz on social media. It seems the message resonated with a lot of people. John DeFilippo, my quarterbacks coach that season, texted me afterward and said, "I read your quote from the press conference, and it gave me chills."

Honestly, I believe the Holy Spirit used me—a weak human vessel—to share an important truth in that moment. It wasn't calculated or prepared. It was just me sharing what I've lived, on the field and off it.

I was drawing from 2 Corinthians 12:9-10 (ESV), one of my favorite Bible passages—the same one I talked about in my YouVersion devotional:

[God] said to me, "My grace is sufficient for you, for my power is made perfect in weakness." Therefore I will boast all the more gladly of my weaknesses, so that the power of Christ may rest upon me. For the sake of Christ, then, I am content with weaknesses, insults, hardships, persecutions, and calamities. For when I am weak, then I am strong.

I am a walking example of the "strength in weakness" principle. My whole career arc bears it out. "Backup quarterback who considered retirement leads team to first Super Bowl"—that's not just a nice underdog story. That's 2 Corinthians 12:9-10 in action!

Tori's struggle with POTS is another example of being at your weakest and needing to trust God every day—even for something like summoning the strength to move from point A to point B..When Tori got sick, we had to dismiss any illusions that we had control over our lives, because at that point, we knew we didn't. There were times when no one else could tell that she was struggling, but even then, her struggle wasn't invisible to God.

Of course, we wish Tori didn't have to go through the constant management of a chronic illness, but over the years, we've seen God use this trial to strengthen our relationship and our faith. This experience has also motivated both of us to get involved with health and nutrition in ways we might not have otherwise. Tori would say that she wouldn't change a thing about the path God led us on. Neither would I.

God is still shaping and refining us. It's not a finished process, by any means. But through everything, our trust in the Lord has grown. And it continues to grow every day.

MY TRUE IDENTITY

During my MVP press conference, I was simply speaking from the heart. I had no expectation that my comments would generate headlines or have the impact they did. Perhaps the reason my response struck a chord with so many people is because it's so different from what we usually hear—especially in professional sports. I could have talked about silencing the critics or proving all the doubters wrong. But what would have been gained by doing that? The truth is, I didn't want to discuss my victories, successes, or honors. I had no interest in dwelling on my own achievements. Everyone saw the game. They knew what happened. I wanted to talk about what they didn't get to see on the field that night—what nobody gets to see. The real secret of my success. So I highlighted my shortcomings and embraced failure as a tool for personal growth.

I didn't want people to think I had everything together just because I'd won a big football game. For one thing, I don't. All your problems don't magically disappear because you have a good day at the office. More importantly, though, I believe that when you share your struggles honestly and transparently, people can relate to you, because everyone has problems. I'm not immune to making mistakes just because I happen to play in the NFL. If anything, I'm even more susceptible to failure. I've thrown a lot of touchdowns in my career, but I've also been picked a bunch of times. I've fumbled the ball, gotten sacked, held on to the ball too long, and made my fair share of boneheaded plays.

Heading into the Super Bowl, I think a lot of people wondered which Nick Foles would show up—the guy who threw for seven touchdowns in one game or the guy who couldn't even get into the red zone against Dallas. The truth is, there's only one Nick Foles, and he's every bit as capable of failure as he is of greatness.

That's the message I wanted to convey during my press conference: no one is perfect. It's okay to stumble, fall, and get back up again. It's okay to admit your faults and flaws and learn from them.

If I hadn't fallen countless times, I wouldn't be where I am today.

Think about it: if I hadn't struggled that first year at Michigan State, I never would have realized how much I needed Jesus in my life. If I hadn't been turned down by all those other schools, I never would have gone to Arizona and met Tori, the love of my life. If I hadn't struggled in St. Louis and walked away from the game, I might never have come to the realization that my identity is not dependent on football. I also never would have gotten a chance to work with Coach Reid again or with Alex. And if Kansas City hadn't opted out of my contract, I never would have ended up back in Philly or been part of the 2017 Eagles. And I wouldn't have won a world championship. One setback leads to a step forward, and we just keep learning and growing. That's how God works.

I've tried to be perfect. I've tried to manage things on my own. I've tried to play the game of life as a one-man team. It just doesn't work. That's how I ended up in the wilderness, both literally and spiritually. But then God graciously led me back and showed me how much stronger I could be if I put my trust in him.

So I'm happy to talk about my weaknesses, struggles, and failures. Because when I do, it highlights the indescribable power of God.

The bottom line is that it's not about me. If I try to make my career or achievements about me, I'm taking the credit away from the one who truly deserves it, the one who made all this possible in the first place. I just want to step out of the way and let people catch a glimpse of God and what he can do.

It still amazes me that the God of the universe loved me enough to sacrifice his own Son on my behalf. I heard the gospel story hundreds of times as a kid. God created human beings. We sinned, and in doing so, we distanced ourselves from God, so God sent his Son to earth to die for us so that we could be saved. It's not about following rules and regulations; it's about believing in Christ and having a personal relationship with him. When I accepted Christ as my personal Savior in that parking lot at Michigan State, my life changed in ways I could never have imagined. But I don't think I ever fully grasped the gravity of what God did for me until I had Lily. To sacrifice your only child to save someone else—as a parent, I find that unimaginable. And yet that's exactly what God did.

Talk about a radical change in perspective. Everything else—the Lombardi included—pales in comparison.

WHO'S IN CHARGE

People always seem to be trying to pin me down to one extreme or the other. I'm either a fluke or a phenom. A leader or a liability. A hoax or a hero. The labels will always be out there, but they don't have the same hold on me that they used to.

Perhaps this has happened to you, too. If so, I want to encourage you to not worry about what other people think. If you do, it will only stunt your own growth and fulfillment. Those influences will start to sway your thoughts and actions, and eventually anxiety will gain a foothold in your heart. The truth is, we all have different gifts, interests, and abilities that God delights in using. Our job is simply to use those gifts in ways that will glorify him and point others toward him.

So whatever crossroads you find yourself at, don't let outside entities write your life story—or even dictate how you perceive it. Proverbs 16:9 says, "We can make our plans, but the LORD determines my steps." He clearly determined mine, and I know he will do the same for you.

It's very humbling. Some days I still don't feel as though I deserve to have been on such a great team and to have won a Super Bowl title.

Then I remind myself that there's a purpose for all of it—the ups and the downs, the failures and the triumphs. Everything has happened so that I could have the opportunity to share the gospel with others.

By the world's standards, my journey from backup quarterback to Super Bowl MVP is almost unbelievable. But right from the very beginning, it was all part of God's master plan. He has been carefully guiding my steps the entire way—occasionally letting me stumble and fall, but always giving me the courage to get back up and keep moving forward.

I'm so grateful that I was given the chance to share my weaknesses, doubts, and fears during that post–Super Bowl press conference. If even one person hears my story and draws closer to God in the process, it will all have been worthwhile.

The Bible says, "God is our merciful Father and the source of all comfort. He comforts us in all our troubles so that we can comfort others. When they are troubled, we will be able to give them the same comfort God has given us" (2 Corinthians 1:3-4).

I hope the comfort I've received through Christ along my journey will be yours, too.

THE FINAL HANDOFF

So, who am I?

I am a football player . . . but that only begins to describe me.

I am a quarterback . . . but my true identity is found in Christ.

I am able to win big games . . . but all the glory goes to God.

I am a Super Bowl MVP . . . but my worth doesn't come from trophies or awards.

I am weak and prone to failure . . . but my Savior covers me in his perfection.

I am Nick Foles, a follower of Christ . . . who just happens to play football at the moment.

Romans 10:9-10 says, "If you openly declare that Jesus is Lord and believe in your heart that God raised him from the dead, you will be saved. For it is by believing in your heart that you are made right with God, and it is by openly declaring your faith that you are saved."

This is the gospel message that changed my life, confirms my identity, and gives me the strength I need for each day. God's saving grace provides me with hope for this life and the one to come. It can do the same for you.

Believe it.

ACKNOWLEDGMENTS

I don't think anyone can prepare you for what it's like to write a book. This was an exciting journey that stretched our faith and abilities. When Tori and I decided we wanted to go through with this project, we agreed to be as transparent and honest as possible. That was difficult at times, but having experienced it, I can say that it has been incredibly rewarding. Through reflecting on both the challenging times and the successful times, I continue to see how present God has been in every roadblock, every accomplishment, and every detour.

I deeply cherish the relationships in my life thus far, because they have impacted me deeply and molded me into the person I am today. Thank you to all my family members, coaches, chaplains, pastors, teammates, and friends. I am grateful for all of you. Though we couldn't get every single person into this book, I hope these stories, thoughts, and passions affect you in a positive and uplifting way.

To the city of Philadelphia and the entire Philadelphia Eagles organization, I am forever thankful to be a part of such a unique team, driven by chemistry and passion. This passion, built on the city we play for, is unlike anything else I've seen.

To the writing team and to the Tyndale publishing team, I am incredibly grateful—specifically, to Josh Cooley and Carol Traver. This project wouldn't have been possible without you and your constant support, hard work, and dedication throughout the process.

When this book came to be, Tori and I prayed about what to do with the proceeds. We truly believe that this journey is the result of none other than God's intervention, and because of that, we feel it's best to give every cent we earn from this book to various churches and organizations that we feel led to be a part of. In doing so, we hope to impact many lives and instill a similar passion in others to give where they feel called.

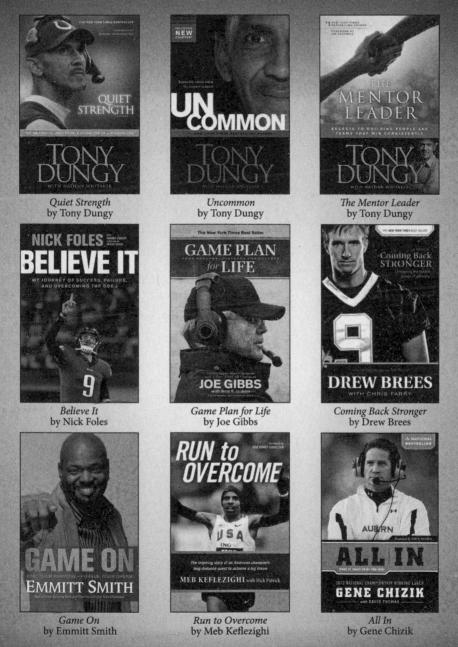